Other Clay

A Remembrance of the World War II Infantry

CHARLES R. CAWTHON

The earth was covered thick with other clay
Which her own clay shall cover, heaped and pent,
Rider and horse — friend, foe, — in one red burial blent!
Waterloo, Lord Byron (1788–1824)

University Press of Colorado

To all those who stayed their course of war
with the 2d Battalion, 116th Regiment (Stonewall Brigade)
29th Infantry Division
6 June 1944–5 May 1945

Copyright © 1990 by the University Press of Colorado
P.O. Box 849, Niwot, CO 80544

Portions of this book were originally published as articles in
American Heritage: The Magazine of History (June 1974, April 1978, and
October/November 1983). Genuine appreciation is given to *American Heritage*
for their permission to reuse the material.

The University Press of Colorado is a cooperative publishing enterprise supported, in part, by Adams State College, Colorado State University, Fort Lewis
College, Mesa State College, Metropolitan State College, University of Colorado, University of Northern Colorado, University of Southern Colorado, and
Western State College.

Quality Printing and Binding by:
Berryville Graphics
P.O. Box 272
Berryville, VA 22611 U.S.A.

Contents

Contents

Prologue

For four years and more, I served in an army infantry battalion in the second of the great world wars of this century. To have been young then and now to be old is personally amazing, for the time lapse seems instantaneous. Early on in those years, this Battalion came to be the close-in boundaries of my world and remained so until its stand-down at the end of the war. With others in it, I shared intense experiences of violence, boredom, exuberance, despair, comedy, and tragedy. In it, too, was spent a prodigious quantity of youth, gone and, of course, irredeemable. Now there remains a pride and nostalgia that lends those years an overall glow they rarely had at the time and, regarded objectively, probably do not deserve.

My battalion was the second of the three of the 116th Regiment (the Stonewall Brigade), 29th Infantry Division. Each was composed of three rifle companies, a weapons company armed with heavy machine guns and mortars, and a Headquarters Company of battalion staff, signal, pioneer, antitank, and transportation platoons. The rifle and weapons companies were designated alphabetically, those of the 2d Battalion being E, F, G, and H, or, in the usage of that war: Easy, Fox, George, and How.

The table of organization called for twenty-eight officers and 900 enlisted men. Rarely was this strength present for duty; combat could reduce it with startling rapidity by a half or more. Until decimated, however, a battalion was capable of effective firepower and maneuvers on its own, the smallest unit of the army so constituted. Self-sufficiency lent a sense of clan and cohesion and made for an efficient organization for performing the irrational acts of war.

By the record, the 2d Battalion performed effectively: It dealt with and absorbed heavy blows; on occasion, it was reduced to a bloodied remnant but, with an infusion of human and materiél replacements — and a few days rest — showed remarkable recuperative powers. Throughout, it retained a definite character, compounded of all who served in it and of all it met.

Upon demobilization, the world of the battalion became as if it had never been, except in the memories of its veterans, who are now departing, file by file, as casually, it seems, as did those who were struck down in battle. Such fading is part of the eternal human sadness, as well as of human renewal. Memorials and memoirs are preservatives of a sort, but these fix, at best, the shadows — often distorted at that — of what has passed.

Nevertheless, as the war ended, I thought to capture, as best I could, the life of my battalion before pervasive oblivion rolled over it. My ill-defined design was on something of a grand scale, embracing the war in the battalion's story. Even briefly advanced, this effort failed to come off for me and, I judged, could hardly do better for a reader. So, I set it aside, convinced that the fault lay with the teller, not the tale.

This failure was contemplated at odd, far-spaced intervals until it dawned that no matter how important and encompassing the battalion's experience was for me, it could hardly embrace a global war. With this belated realization, I wrote a narrow firsthand account of the battalion's Saint-Lô battle, and it turned out very well. Then, there came to hand two Civil War memoirs that, in style and content, marked what should be the flanks of my own effort. One of these is John Overton Cassler's *Four Years in the Stonewall Brigade.* In this brief volume, Private Cassler ingeniously captured an image of the ranks of his brigade of 1861–1865.

The other, *I Rode with Stonewall,* is by Henry Kyd Douglas, who may have been the most personable and articulate soldier in the Southern armies. Douglas was a keen observer and a faithful recorder. The scenes and conversations that he preserved are among the most graphic we have of the men and women who fed the brief flame of the Confederacy from its first fierce light to its smoldering end.

Cassler's and Douglas's four years of war were far harder than mine. Their battles started practically upon mobilization; they endured incomparably greater privation throughout. The ultimate difference, however, lay in the overwhelming odds they faced, and in the approach and devastating presence of defeat that they experienced. Each, in his own sphere and style — private soldier and enterprising staff officer, tells his story without self-pity or mock heroics. The military level of my own account, set in a vastly different war and time, falls somewhere between these two. In the telling, I follow their example as best I can, bearing in mind Douglas's self-admonishment to "write soberly, discreetly, and fairly."

With my two preceptors I have in common starting war as a rank amateur, in the company of others equally amateur. Each in our four-year span learned and practiced the violent profession of ground combat and lost friends whose like we never found again.

So much for the late date and form of this memoir. The personal background to it is not extensive. I was born and reared in Murfreesboro, a Middle Tennessee town most notable at that time as the site of a major Civil War battle that had raged along the banks of Stones River, just outside its meager limits, around New Year's Day, 1863. The battle was still a presence in the town when I was a boy, its memory revived annually at reunions of the county's Confederate veterans. My father, born and reared in Murfreesboro during the Reconstruction, was active in organizing these gatherings of shrunken and palsied old men who huddled in their gray uniforms under the great oaks at the fairgrounds each spring to hear themselves lauded once again for long-lost battles. I recall the pungent smell of sides of shoat and kid roasted all night over pits of hickory coals, the warmth of early spring, and oratory that had, undoubtedly, a high content of bathos. Nonetheless, the reunions pulsed with a vitality and emotion that even a boy who understood little of what it was all about could feel and long remember. This, and a pastime of wandering over the half-century-old battlefield, hunting the conical lead slugs (Minié balls) with which the North and South had argued their differences, constituted my military background until 1940.

In the interim, I finished college at what is now Middle Tennessee State University, in the midst of the Great Depression and started as a $5-a-week reporter on the Murfreesboro *News Journal.* Two years later, I moved on to Virginia and was with the *Bulletin* newspaper in Martinsville, and then was editor of the Charlottesville *Daily Progress*. During that period the war began and moved step by inexorable step to engulf Europe. The United States began thinking the unthinkable possibility of involvement. Selective service became law, and mobilization of the National Guard was decreed. Looking back, this was a remarkably hardheaded decision for the Republic to take. None of the traditional inspirations to war were present: We were not actively threatened and had neither revenge nor the desire for territorial gain to exalt and sanctify the martial spirit. On the contrary, the national memory of 1914–1918, when Europe had last blown itself up to no lasting purpose, was still heavy and sour. This war — sequel to that horror — looked even uglier, especially in its momentary alliance between Nazi Germany and the communist Soviet Union. Apart from small, passionately committed groups agitating on the Allied and Axis sides, the whole business engendered more distaste than fervor.

There was no lack of patriotism, or of that young men's spirit of adventure in which war-fever germinates so readily, but these emotions were not hyperstimulated as in 1861, 1898, and 1917. Having read of the wild excitement of those years, I wondered at its lack but, in keeping with the emotional climate of the time, gave more thought to the fact that, being a young unmarried male, I was prime material for what the law decreed was to be one year of military service.

This prospect focused my attention on an announcement by the Virginia National Guard of an Officer Candidate School (OCS) to fill out its complement of second lieutenants for mobilization; a much preferable way, it seemed, to spend a year in the army. In order to apply, I enlisted in Martinsville's H Company (heavy weapons) of the 116th Regiment.

I was accepted for the OCS and reported at the Hotel Murphy in Richmond, where it was held, early in December 1940. For two weeks, we one hundred or so candidates toiled at and were tested on elementary map-reading, army organization, military justice, chemical warfare, guard duty, and drill. Our day's work ran from 7:30 A.M. to 10:30 P.M., or, reckoning by the military's twenty-four-hour clock, from 0730 to 2230; the material was not difficult, but there was much of it. Although considerable tension was generated over acceptance or rejection, few were winnowed out; the demand for second lieutenants of infantry, to become all-consuming as the war developed, was already ominously great.

In any event, the State of Virginia, "reposing special trust and confidence in [my] patriotism, valor, fidelity and abilities," commissioned me to military command — presumably in battle, though assurances continued that combat for American youth was not to be. I was authorized to wear a single gold bar on each shoulder of my uniform, and the infantry insignia of crossed rifles — proudly depreciated as "idiot sticks" — on the lapels.

Never has the Republic leaned even so lightly upon a greener reed, or on one more conscious of his greenness. Otherwise, I was healthy, bookishly inclined, and as yet unaware of a latent paternal feeling for those who came under my care. I had, too, it developed, some ability at dissembling the fear, uncertainty, and irritability that the war, in general, inspired.

Now, as to sources: first, memory, notoriously unreliable, erratic, and subject to afterthought — all defects that become more pronounced with time. Documents are in somewhat better case. My first attempt at this account, though abbreviated, can be considered as documentary, for it was written when the deep impressions of the sights, sounds, and smells of 1941–1945 were fresh. It was based upon notes made while in hospital during the winter of 1944–1945. Wartime letters, which my admiring mother stored in chronological order in shoe boxes, are also a monitor. Censorship, and a due regard for a mother's capacity for worry, make these letters monumentally banal, but they help illuminate dim recollections of times and places. Dogeared pocket notebooks in which I scribbled the edicts of superiors and notes for my own pronouncements are another source, forming something of a bare-bones diary. Amazingly, a smudged notation — *Breakfast 0500 cross IP 0600* — can evoke a scene, decades past, of a sleep-sodden column lurching toward some point in the infinity of time and space. Failure to bring men and geographic point together on the moment would draw for their commander a sharp rebuke. The simple jargon also throws back echoes of the clink and creak of equipment, crunch of boots on gravel, and a moving frieze of darker shapes against a general autumn darkness.

Again aiding memory are the army's "green books," the official record of the war practically hour by hour. More personal is the division's history,

29 Let's Go by Joseph H. Ewing, an infantry platoon leader in our 175th Regiment, who wrote with firsthand feeling. Closer still to home is the 2d Battalion's unit journal, a record of where we were and what we were doing from D-day on. The entries are erratic and often without significance, an infantry battalion in combat not being conducive to thoughtful composition. Parts of the journal were lost as its keeping passed from recorder to recorder down the casualty list. That it survives is due to the late Andrew McFazden of battalion headquarters, who recognized it as something of value and salvaged pages that otherwise would have disappeared.

The recollections of comrades are another cross-check on my own. Their faces, forms, and voices are in the fabric of my account. Not many are identified by name, for time and the fact that few outside our close circle ever knew us makes names incidental; there is no significance to who is named or who is not.

A memoir is a personal appearance in which one is inclined to stand straighter and present the best profile. Mitigating this tendency, I have no deeds of personal daring to relate, and no action of mine had a discernible effect on the war. Numerically and actually, of all Americans in uniform I was about a one–fourteen-millionth part. My observations are limited to what could be seen from the about six-feet level of my eyes (often lower, for I found war much less disturbing from ground level or below). Even within this close horizon, some persons and happenings undoubtedly appear larger than life, while others of more significance were missed altogether. In sum, I write of the trivia of life and death in a tight, violent, and brief-lived little world. This is not to belittle it; military victory was decisive. In closing the books on this aspect of the war, such trivia in sum spell the end result of grand designs and great stratagems. The war's political, economic, and social account books, of course, have not yet been closed and probably never will be, for entries have continued to pile up and have become so entangled as to defy audit.

Returning to my narrow narrative path, I do not know how closely what I relate parallels the experiences of other foot soldiers. Our superiors made a great difference to our separate fates, not only by reason of their professional abilities, but also by the performance they required. And, as always, blatant chance, with an exceptional range of geography and foes available to it, had great sport with us all.

By cross section of human material, all army infantry battalions must have been much alike and should be recognizable to one another, for each was assembled by largely random selection from the nation's manpower. Make no mistake about it, however, each man's war is separate and personal unto himself and not exactly like that of any other. It is fought first within his own heart and soul, and the outcome is buried with his bones.

Finally, I have said that a memoir is a thing of lingering shadows of people and events past. Some of the shadows that I probe here are etched into memory as sharply as those scorched into the bridge abutments and pavements at Hiroshima by the atomic blast. Others are wavering and faint forms glimpsed at a distance in a twilight. I grope toward them to see more clearly, and they retreat further into the mists, seemingly more in regret than in mockery at having so to remind me that the brief substance of all this passed by long ago.

1

And So It Began

> The die had been cast; the lines drawn; the decree had gone forth, and no mortal hand could stay the tempest or arrest the calamity.
>
> *Four Years in the Stonewall Brigade* (1861–1865)
> John O. Cassler

On the morning of 3 February 1941, H Company, Virginia National Guard, Martinsville, Virginia, mustered in its armory and was sworn into active federal service. It was not a stirring scene; no bands played, no crowds cheered. Only a thin formation of less than one hundred young men stood in ranks in a high-girded hall that doubled as the town's ballroom. It was a gathering more notable than it appeared, or I knew. Over the next four years, most of those men — uniformed and armed then largely as their fathers had been in a war twenty-four years before — would be killed or wounded. Counting out those who never made it to the battle, the attrition was nearly total.

Company officers stood in a group to one side while platoon sergeants called rolls of names that could not have varied greatly in arrangement of vowels and consonants from those sounded when the Stonewall Brigade companies mustered for the Civil War. It was a litany, a plainsong with Anglo-Saxon and Celtic roots. As the war ground on, surnames of Polish, German, Italian, Spanish, French, and Slavic origin appeared on the rolls, and the company became more generally mid-20th–century American. For the moment, however, it was all Virginia-town of a lengthening time ago. Its like will not be assembled again, for the conditions that produced it are too far removed ever to return. The United States in 1941 was still a relatively uncrowded country with upward of 100 million fewer bodies than in this last decade of the century. The 130 million or so population of those days was, I think, about the optimum ratio of people to space and to resources, as yet unstrained. It was a country just emerging from the Great Depression, which had been, also, a great social homogenizer and leveler, for all had felt its bite. Years of serious want, however, had not changed a strong belief in the general superiority of things American, and a confidence that the world would be better if it were more as we were.

My concern on that particular morning, however, was not with economic depression or with nationalism, but with what I should do as the roll call ended Captain Howard Minter, the company commander, told us to take our posts. I had been assigned to the antitank platoon, which so far had no weapons. At its front stood the direct-eyed Sergeant Clyde England, and, not knowing what else to do, I strode toward him. He showed a bare glint of amusement as he saluted and retired to the ranks; I took his place, feeling more alone than ever before and seldom since. Any command presence could have been only outward; inwardly, I was under the direct control of doubt as to what I should do, and as to why I was there in the first place.

Whatever else the platoon may have thought of its new leader, it had good reason to wonder at his uniform, which included riding pants, boots, and spurs, though a horse had not been on the company property books for over twenty years. This garb, so remotely related to that ordained, was the result of wartime shortages that were already surfacing in a doubling and redoubling army. After three months' effort, I still had not a complete infantry officer's uniform; the pants and boots were a loan from Captain Minter, who saw this as the only alternative to having one of his officers mustered into service in civilian slacks.

The following days did little to lighten dark doubts over having sought a commission to perform duties for which I was so sketchily trained, and for which I began to think I had little aptitude. The daily calisthenics and touch football were familiar, and, at close-order drill, I could imitate more experienced hands well enough to get by, but in weapons training and the more involved subjects, I was behind all but the newest recruits. There was no way to fake it and little opportunity for private study. The paperwork required to send the American soldier off to war occupied every evening.

The company was quartered in the armory and took meals, under contract, at a downtown restaurant, marching the several blocks three times each day in cold, dank, February weather. The townspeople paid little heed to this martial display, even when we counted the march step in unison, making a brave sound echoing off the buildings. It was as if the uniformed young men of the town had no connection with the headlines about the devastating air blitz of London or the fighting in North Africa, then under way. The ladies of a church did give us a dinner one night and asked in return that the company sing "God Bless America," which we did in a heavy rumble.

Altogether, it was a strange mobilization, but if our lads felt they were being shorted the traditional status of hero, they did not show it. The majority had been in the company for some years simply because they liked soldiering, fitting the category described by General George Washington as having a "natural fondness for military parade."

Others, like myself, were highly eligible for the draft and had chosen this as a better alternative. Our attitude, overall, was a simple acceptance of the inevitable. My own stoicism was diluted by the fact that between OCS and induction I had been hired as editor of the Charlottesville, Virginia, *Daily Progress* — by far my longest step upward to date. I was anxious to finish the military year and test the Selective Service Act's provision that I would then get my job back.

After two crowded and confused weeks at the armory, the company was ordered to assemble with the rest of the 116th Regiment and the 29th Division at Fort Meade, Maryland, one of the cluster of military installations around the District of Columbia. The company made the move by train; commissioned and noncommissioned officers (NCOs) owning cars were authorized to drive through. Thus I met my first real hazard of the war, for Captain Minter, a nervous and fastidious man, kept us up all the previous night preparing for an early-morning departure. As a result, I drove the last of the long day's journey half asleep and in the midst of convoys of army trucks converging on the fort.

3

The cantonment area of Fort Meade in February 1941 was not a joy to behold. Everything had a flayed look; unpainted wooden barracks sprouted in rows out of vast, rutted, sandy fields, and cleared vegetation was bulldozed into huge piles, all under a dull, gray-glass sky that threatened snow. Here we stayed through a long winter, spring, and sweltering summer — all seasons of equal discontent that fed on a feeling of lack of purpose as the government continued to assure the country that its sons would not go to war.

Winter weather and barracks living sent many to the hospital. Schools and special assignments took officers and NCOs away, and often I was left alone to conduct training with little equipment and less knowledge. Uncertainty about the wisdom of having sought a commission continued strong, especially when standing at predawn reveille in the freezing slush while, in the distance, the regimental band played "Over the Rainbow" to the accompaniment of coughing and sneezing in the ranks behind me.

This alone, however, is too bleak a picture. We new lieutenants were young, and enough in the same boat so that friendships came easily. Caught between the oft-expressed disapproval of senior officers and of the ranks (who, while not vocal about it, also recognized our shortcomings), we led a clannish and sometimes hilarious existence. It was, I suppose, an adequate mill for grinding out wartime officers for the Republic.

I was fortunate in that the irritable Captain Minter ran a tight company, even though he was there little of the time. Discipline was no problem, and by obviously trying to learn the job, I got on well enough with men who, with amazing patience, accepted this in lieu of professional competence.

When chance threw my lot with the 116th, I had not known that it was the direct descendant of the 2d Virginia Regiment of the legendary Stonewall Brigade of the Civil War, which, until it was fought and marched to extinction, may well have been the most deadly single formation of infantry that this country — North or South — has produced. A regiment, is no more inclined than is an individual to forswear a title won by an illustrious ancestor. We claimed, without qualm, this one that had been won eighty years before when the brigade stood "like a stone wall" on Henry House Hill, above the waters of Bull Run and under the blaze of Yankee fire and a July sun, to turn the tide of battle.

Having been reared on Civil War lore, especially of the rebel side, I was vastly impressed to find myself a "Stonewaller." I had trouble, though, relating my fumbling efforts and those of the largely bored soldiers around me to the legendary fierce gray ghosts of the Army of Northern Virginia. Panting through morning calisthenics and a run around the company area did not give much feeling of kinship with soldiers about whom Private Cassler wrote: "The laws of the human body seemed to have been reversed for these men. They fought and marched and triumphed like war machines which felt no need for rest, or food, or sleep. In one day they marched from Harpers Ferry to Strasburg, nearly 50 miles."

For my efforts as a second lieutenant I received $125 each month, and shelter in an unpainted, pine-walled cell, furnished with chair and cot. There was also a food allowance of $18 a month. Even in uninflated currency, this did not allow for riotous living. Uniform was a major expense; boots, it seemed, wore out faster than I could buy them. A modest weekend away from Fort Meade could leave me short of money for a haircut.

Spring, as I recall, came early that year of 1941. The violated earth of the cantonment area was raked and smoothed, and everything else was painted. Here and there, grass showed, and the few battered trees that had survived the builders launched their leaves. The war was running amuck: The British had apparently won the air battle over their isles; the German armies had turned to the east and were massing on the borders of the Soviet Union, unknown to us and, apparently, ignored by Stalin.

Whatever was involving Stalin's attention that spring, H Company was occupied with eighty-one draftees who arrived to fill out its ranks. This was before the basic training camps were established, and the new men had come directly from induction centers. To initiate members into a society always stimulates interest; spirits picked up as they were drilled and told about the tough winter the company had been through. They seemed suitably impressed, and it was generally agreed that this was "the best bunch of boys, ever."

The hot, humid weather of the mid-Atlantic coastal plain came on, and the novelty of imparting knowledge to novices, seeing new faces, and hearing new tales quickly palled. The company reverted to a unified interest in weekend passes and in finishing the year of service. I shared these interests but managed not to be vocal about it. There was no awareness that time was ticking inexorably toward war, or that when it came, the days of battle would terminate life for so many.

Not all was grousing and lack of spirit. Lieutenant Colonel Edley Craighill, the 2d's commander, was a top-flight soldier, veteran of the 1918 war, and from a family long connected with the regiment. He felt deeply about its traditions, and this enthusiasm impelled us, to a lesser degree, along with him. In a maneuver in July, we covered nine miles in little more than three hours of forced marching in heat and road dust. The colonel then decided that we were ready for real "foot cavalry" work and so led a 32-mile march over the back roads of Maryland. We started out strongly, early on a summer's morning, and the column grew progressively more silent as the heat mounted and the miles multiplied. The bulk of the battalion came in some twelve hours later, considerably butt-sprung but still with some spirit. Such efforts left me feeling something less than one of Private Cassler's "war machines," but, I told myself, the incentives were different: This was not the Valley Campaign, the march to cut off Pope at Second Manassas or to reach the rear of the Yankee army at Chancellorsville. The inimitable "Stonewall" was a long-ago legend, and a legend loses impact in the presence of a scorching July sun and weary legs.

Early on, as an amateur foot soldier, I regarded the long road march as deadly dull and of little use in the age of gasoline motors. Later, in the light of battle experience, I realized that the guts to take one more step long after the body signals its impossibility is — along with the will always to take one more shot — the essence of the foot soldier. For this, the long, hard road march — just plain footslogging — is the specific. It was also known in my war as the "separator": the best precombat "separator of the men from the boys." I trust that no matter how many armored personnel carriers it acquires, the army never gives up the regular twenty–thirty-mile (or more) road march, no matter the weather, as training for which there is no substitute.

Summer wore on; the sandy, scrub-grown training areas of Fort Meade were without comfort. Attrition, that was to assume such awesome levels in battle, began tentative forays. Now, its principal toll was among officers of World War I vintage. The bottle also took a few. Youth, and an acceptable level of sobriety, moved up; so far, there were few losses from faint heart.

The senior command of the regiment remained firm. At its head was Colonel E. W. Opie, publisher of the Staunton, Virginia, newspaper, a soldier with moral impact in inverse proportion to his erect, slightly built frame. I paid him the tribute I reserved for forceful and exacting commanders who did not appreciate my slam-bang approach to command: I stayed out of his way. He suffered neither fools nor indolence.

A mainstay of the staff was the adjutant, Captain Tom Howie: athletic, courageous, and an incurably kindly hearted gentleman. I met him on my first tour as officer of the day when I reported for instructions and asked where serious transgressors were to be confined.

"Lieutenant," he said seriously and instructively, "the 116th does not have a guardhouse. You have only to remind our soldiers of who they are to bring them into line."

Before the night was over, I had to take a guard detail to subdue a burly drunk who was running amuck in a barracks. I do not recall what we did with him, but I do know that soon the 116th had a guardhouse with as full a complement of prisoners as any.

Tom may have changed his opinion of the responsiveness to regimental pride of all whom chance brought into our ranks, but he remained idealistic and kind in an environment hostile to both qualities. If this tale has an individual hero, it is this soldier whose character would better have become us all. I caught another glimpse of this one wintery Sunday afternoon when he came by my cell on the lieutenants' floor with a telegram from a young lady — this at a time when captains largely ignored lieutenants, except to correct them. The telegram was innocent enough, but Tom knew that on the lieutenants' floor nothing connected with young women was construed as innocent. (It was standard practice that whoever answered our single telephone yelled out: "Lieutenant _____. Miss _____ says she must see you at once!" Tom Howie would not subject even a second lieutenant to embarrassment, so, when the open telegram came across his desk, he delivered it himself rather than entrust it to the officer of the day. He is the one of our regiment on whom the twilight of war has lingered longest — a matter for later telling.

By the end of six months of active duty, three broad categories of the diverse personalities that made up the officer corps of the 116th had sorted themselves out: Most conspicuous were the few who, being arbitrary and demanding by nature, found in military service an ideal climate. These talked considerably about being "hard but fair." It is possible that they did have some special insight into fairness, but on looking back, I cannot discern it. In any event, they appeared to prosper most in an atmosphere that became progressively harsher. At the opposite end were the few of a naturally kindly nature who underwent no war change. They were not weak or incompetent, for the weak and incompetent did not last long enough to form a category, but they had a durable idealism and consideration that stood up under a constant battering. The majority of us were at times arbitrary and then again lenient, and under disturbingly similar circumstances. We were often unsure as to where fairness lay and worried considerably about our inconsistencies. It seems to me that the stream of officers that passed through the regiment over the next four years all fit into one or another of these molds, with some overlapping.

The NCOs also fitted roughly into the same patterns as, perhaps, did the rest of the regiment. All of us were mixed together in variations and combinations that are wonderful to recall.

When the caps began to pop on Omaha Beach, the useful human qualities came down to just two: outward, if not inward, calm, and courage. No degree of human toughness, either natural or forced, could match that of the indiscriminate bullet or shell fragment. My observation is that calm and courage surfaced fully as frequently among the gentle as among the harsh, and that those in the middle group — true to their nature — were sometimes one and sometimes the other. I am convinced that there is no consistent connection between being outwardly tough and inwardly courageous, despite a tendency to equate the two.

In September, the division traveled by truck convoy to the first Carolina maneuvers, involving two army corps, the traditional "Red Army" and "Blue Army" of practice war. The maneuvers covered vast stretches of piedmont, whose sun-bleached and still economically depressed towns and farms were much like my native heath. The maneuvers, at my level, were a huge, uncomfortable, motorized camping trip. The antitank platoon, now equipped with inadequate 50-caliber machine guns, shifted from place to place, ostensibly protecting the 2d Battalion from trucks bearing signs designating them as "tanks," which never appeared. The top commanders and staffs that supplied and ordered us about may have received useful training, but I learned nothing I did not already know about breathing dust and sleeping on the ground.

The emphasis was on motorized mobility, stemming, apparently, from an impression that the German army's sweeps across Poland, Western Europe, and, now, Russia were accomplished almost entirely on wheels and tracks; this despite the news photos of long, toiling columns of foot soldiers. In any event, during that fall of 1941, we rode about in dust-covered convoys, dismounting occasionally for reasons unclear to a platoon leader, and then mounting again to ride some more. If modern war were fought on wheels, with Detroit, dominant in the motor field, on our side, we would win hands down.

In many such ways, our training was for a "never-never" war; the first shock of combat made it appear to have been playing at cops and robbers. There was great emphasis on motor-march discipline. H Company came a cropper on the first day out of Fort Meade. We missed a checkpoint right under the hard eye of the divisional commander, who promptly restricted Tom Dallas, by then commanding the company, to quarters for the weekend. Few other memories remain sharp; one — and one of my lasting impressions of the Great War — is of riding several hundred miles in a solid-sprung command car while seated on a boil. Another is taking my platoon for a swim after a hot, dusty day in the trucks and being absent when Tom Dallas, returning from a commanders' conference, assembled the company to set forth the next day's operations. This upset him considerably, and I was restricted to quarters for the weekend. Tom was big in body, heart, and temper, surviving the war to die in an army helicopter crash in Alaska. He saved my ignorant and sometimes indolent skin on a number of occasions. Later, I accused him of having restricted me because I had had a swim and he had not; at the moment, I remained very quiet.

Vendors of ice cream, candy, cold drinks, and tobacco trailed the columns wherever we went, charging exorbitant prices in the larcenous tradition of the army sutler. They were as tenacious as ticks and, with the connivance of the troops, managed to stick with us despite the ire of commanders who suspected them of being agents employed by maneuvers enemies.

Also following the flag through the hot Carolina autumn was a sizable contingent of wives and sweethearts, also motorized, there being as yet no gasoline rationing. These loyal — and, I dare say, custodial-minded — souls took seedy lodgings wherever they could be found and located their men through some extrasensory process. Viewed from on high, we must all have presented a scene as old as war: a dust-raising army and its dusty followers, with the modern touch of motor propulsion rather than hoof and foot. Many Americans, now in middle age, are no doubt Carolinians by conception, if not by birth.

Maneuvers terminated for me in early November, when I was assigned to a three-month course for company grade officers at the Infantry School, Fort Benning, Georgia. I left the truck-riding over Carolina without regret. The nights were turning cold, and we were denied the privilege of burning fence rails that Sherman's columns had enjoyed on their marches through the country seventy-five years before. Repair crews, rather than carpetbaggers, trailed our moves to fix any damage we might do.

I retrieved my car from storage and drove down to Benning, which covers a great tract of the sand hills of western Georgia. Columbus is the capital of Fort Benning and, during the war years, Phoenix City, over the line in Alabama, was its fallen girlfriend.

The Infantry School was hyperactive, swarming with officer candidates and officer students on crash courses that, it was hoped, would supply the army with competent leadership. The students were organized into companies of lieutenants, each with a captain-student in charge. My company proved an unruly bunch, representing practically every regiment in the army. Although they may have behaved very well in their own outfits, a number took unabashed advantage of our hapless and overweight captain's lack of force to make his life miserable. His only recourse for obtaining some sort of order as we marched to and from classes and demonstrations was to command, "At*tent*ion!" Whereupon the loud comments and ribald suggestions from the ranks would be stilled for the moment but soon resumed. Some of us felt sorry for the captain but also annoyed with him and ashamed of the example we set in passing other smartly stepping formations of officer candidates. The ten months we had been through had taught, if nothing else, that there is no help for the officer who will not use the leverage of command; our disapproval must have added to his troubles.

Classes were held on an assembly-line basis. The lethal subjects of tactics, weapons, and chemical warfare were presented enthusiastically or matter-of-factly, depending upon the temperament of the instructor. The major who conducted bayonet instruction was particularly vehement, as, I suppose, he should have been. He laid great and loud stress upon the aggressive spirit imbued by the bayonet, while a demonstration team showed the various moves for efficiently skewering an enemy or battering his brains out with the rifle butt. I am not sure that he imbued the class with anything more than a determination to avoid a bayonet fight, if possible.

Time ticked down to 7 December 1941, a day that seemed accompanied by a sudden crash of cymbals and thundering roll of drums that were to continue, muted or at crescendo, through the next four years. The sounds still reverberate in the memories of the generation that heard them firsthand, though for later generations it may all be as remote and academic as the Minutemen's rifle fire at Lexington, or that first shell that arched, streaming sparks, from the battery at Charleston across the bay toward Fort Sumter.

For me, as for many another of the generation of that time and place, the sounds of Pearl Harbor are a point from which to measure many things before and after. The time was midafternoon of a bright, brisk, early-winter day in southern Georgia; the place was the polo field at Fort Benning, watching two now-forgotten teams at man's immemorial play — contending over a ball. The feel of the sun was pleasant, as was the sight of patterned movements of men, horses, and mallets. Then the shock waves from detonating bombs six thousand miles away passed down the line of onlookers. The polo game went on to an unnoticed conclusion while we hovered around car radios, snatching at the fragmentary and largely repetitious reports from which could be gathered that war had come upon us disastrously and from a quarter we had not expected, though it is apparent now that there had been warning enough. A war results, it appears, from a collusion of miscalculations on both sides, and proceeds and ends through a continuation of the same process.

By the close of that Sunday, we realized that any previous life plans were invalidated. Where we were now headed was too immense and unknowable to grasp, so we students settled upon the comprehensible worry of whether Christmas leave would be canceled. The higher direction of Fort Benning was apparently beset by the same problem — what to concern itself with in the vast spectrum available — and fixed on blackout of the reservation as being at hand and attainable. The response of the Philippines command, six hours after the attack, was to leave its aircraft lined up on Clark Field for the Japanese to blast into oblivion and thus conclude their one-day crippling sweep of U.S. sea and air power in the Pacific.

So, from concern about Christmas leave to military insanity and chaos, and with infinite variations in between, the United States reacted to a war that now encircled the globe. It seems to me that our desire to get home for Christmas was as practical a response as any under the circumstances.

Within a few days, common sense regrouped to some extent after its rout of 7 December. The Benning blackout was dropped with the realization that even had the Japanese and Germans wanted to waste bombs on so unremunerative a patch of Georgia, it was thousands of miles beyond the range of their planes. Leave for students was authorized; there was little we could do about the disasters at Pearl Harbor and Clark Field except to second-guess them.

So, I spent the first wartime Christmas at home. John Rucker, a boyhood friend who was in OCS at Benning, and I drove through most of a night to Murfreesboro. It was a holiday overhung by the debacle already taking shape in the Philippines. My mother, sister, and I visited Father's grave; on Sunday, we occupied the usual pew at the First Presbyterian Church; on Christmas morning, we exchanged presents. I managed to visit my old colleagues of the *Daily News Journal* to allow admiration of my uniform. All of this may sound precious today, but it was the way of life of Middle America in 1941.

Then, on a bleak December day, I drove out to the old Stones River Civil War battlefield to see if my military experience lent any better understanding of what had happened there seventy-eight years before. All I saw, however, were frozen, stubbled fields of corn and cotton stalks, and the dark green cedars. The only evidence of the blood that had been spilled on these fields was a national cemetery, a few monuments, and brush-grown remnants of earthworks where, as a boy, I had played at war. It was a brooding setting, but somehow I still could not imagine the swaying lines of men, spouting death and destruction at each other in that bitter arena. I concluded that a year of military service had not given me a very vivid concept of battle.

After a week, John Rucker and I returned to Benning. I was not to see my family again for four years.

The course ended in February with brief graduation ceremonies and award of certificates attesting to our basic knowledge of modern killing methods. It is doubtful that many of the class who got to the point of applying those lessons survived the process. I arrived back at Fort Meade to hear the company's tales of anti-invasion exercises and coast-watching for infiltrating agents. Strangely, it did not seem at all illogical that we should guard against the contingency of the Germans pulling armies out of the middle of Russia, crossing the Atlantic in winter, and invading our East Coast. War, from a distance, has aspects of a Mad Hatter's tea party attended by manic-depressives quaffing a hallucinatory beverage. Its redeeming features are courage, some selflessness, and moments of gallantry and true nobility — all in all, a baffling business.

The draft shifted into high gear as the country went on total war footing. In March, the 29th received some five thousand of the new levies and formed them into a separate regiment for basic training. I was in charge of one of the training battalions and began again the now-familiar routine of instruction in drill and weaponry, with the equally familiar shortages in equipment. For the entire battalion, there was a single 81-millimeter (mm) mortar and, typical of our instructive straits, a sergeant explaining to recruits crowded onto a barracks floor how the sharp velocity of a mortar round propelled from the tube retracted a pin and armed the round; that was as close as the new men got to a mortar. Marching and yelling, however, were in good supply, so we marched and yelled at them and in general made their lives uncomfortable, all on the basis, as they were frequently and unnecessarily reminded, that there was a war on. They displayed neither fervor for battle nor resentment of the uncomfortable and dangerous job to which they were being put. Perhaps the depression had conditioned us all to an acceptance of things as we found them. Griping and grousing developed along with the training, but it was the normal relief of a soldier's emotional pressure, much as the belch was a relief to his digestive system from the pressures generated by army food.

The training cycle ended, and the recruits were assigned throughout the division. Those we had received the previous spring had been from Virginia, but these were from all over the eastern seaboard and diluted the Virginian cast of the Stonewall Brigade, including its accent. The change was not to any disadvantage that I ever experienced.

In mid-April, the division moved to Camp A. P. Hill, which the government had created just below Fredericksburg, Virginia, by preempting most of a county and dispossessing its inhabitants. We had trained at A. P. Hill the previous summer, just after it was opened, and had found its mosquitoes and underbrush formidable. Now, it had been heavily used for a year; closed latrine pits and kitchen sumps had proliferated, and it was beginning to have the lived-in look of a hobo jungle. Spring heat, interspersed with thundering rains, did not enhance the tent camps. In May, Tom Dallas was assigned to the senior course at the Infantry School, and I fell heir to H Company, though not joyfully. I felt I had reached my level of military competence with a platoon and would have been content to stay there for what would now be the duration. I did not, however, decline the command.

Everything was changing so rapidly under the whip of war that six months before was considered the "old days" of the regiment. To the departures of the aged and the alcohol cases were now added the cadres levied for the new divisions being organized and the assignments of NCOs to OCS. Fortunately for me, some of the best of H Company's NCOs elected not to apply, though they would have made good officers.

Training, too, was changing. It was now realized that the bulk of the German armies did not ride most of the time, after all, but moved and fought on foot. So, back we went to footslogging.

In early June, the 116th paraded in Washington to inspire government workers to greater efforts. We tramped down Constitution Avenue in columns of battalions (something the Civil War Stonewall Brigade would have been delighted to do) and, for soldiers who had been living in the dust and mud, made a very good show. The thin crowd along the sidewalks applauded perfunctorily; noticeably absent was the wild enthusiasm that I had expected from the tales of such parades in World War I.

The emotional pattern of the war was taking shape: There were the trappings of bands, massive rallies, banners, and oratory, but in the ranks there was little of "Cheer, boys, cheer" and "Rally 'round the flag." The World War II soldier, on the whole, I believe, went to the battlefield more at the urging of duty and sober conviction. The challenge of Pearl Harbor was unqualified. The war grew out of a welter of political and economic conflicts, but for the soldier, it all boiled down to the fact that a mortal blow had been aimed at his country and survival was at stake. After the first shock and defiant rage were over, it seems to me, the nation settled down to an all-out determined effort, conducted with remarkable efficiency, dedication, sacrifice, and courage. There were also periods and places of white-hot fervor, but this was not constant or universal. The depths of sorrow for the dead were plumbed, and the elation of victory savored. The scene would not be complete without the profiteers and cheats who always surface at such an opportunity.

War-waging emotion is reflected in the music it inspires. Nothing of the thundering power of the "Battle Hymn of the Republic" of 1861–1865 emerged in 1941–1945. The most abiding song, "America the Beautiful," was actually composed by Irving Berlin in 1919 and was not accepted by the nation until the late, great Kate Smith sang it in 1938, as the war clouds were gathering, much bigger than a man's hand, over Europe. "White Christmas" remains a popular holiday song, but it is evocative of wartime only to those of that generation. All the rest, such as "Milkman Keep Those Bottles Quiet" (in effect, the plea of the well-paid defense worker for undisturbed sleep), "Don't Sit Under the Apple Tree," and "Boogie-Woogie Bugle Boy," have a lilt; those such as "I'll Be Seeing You," fit well the sadly sentimental wartime genre, but all are heard now only at anniversaries, which are, themselves, becoming more widely spaced. So, it seems to me, the songs we sang fit the war we fought and will disappear with us.

After we returned to A. P. Hill, we made marches, on successive days, of twenty and seventeen miles, and along the way, I picked up a touch of "camp stomach" that probably did not help my disposition. Again, not all was discomfort or discontent. A balmy evening in late June found the battalion sprawled along a grassy hillside awaiting orders to move back to camp after an all-day exercise. The site formed a natural amphitheater, its ceiling hung with stars and a full moon. Wagner, the mimic from E Company, took the stage and, with a little urging from the ranks, began imitating commanders. He did Colonel Opie inveighing forcefully against cooks chopping firewood before reveille, and against "naked torsos" — the colonel's term for soldiers appearing outside their tents without shirts. In such ways it was an antique army. Wagner then did Colonel Craighill on "precision and esprit," and moved on to the vocal habits of the company commanders, mine being, "Let's go, H!" I had not realized how often I used that phrase, or how stridently, or how good a mirror is a mimic. The battalion caught every nuance and roared its approval.

The whistles blew, and we formed up and marched away down the moonlit track through the soft Virginia night and the green smells of spring, the ranks still laughing and telling each other that Wagner was "sure enough a good one." An outfit without its Wagners is missing an essential element, even though it is not one listed on the tables of equipment. The 2d Battalion was fortunate in usually having several on hand.

There was less happiness a week or so later over rival claims for places in the 50 percent of the company to be authorized passes over the Fourth of July holiday, the last before the second Carolina maneuvers started. Using a complex formula, involving those due to depart for OCS and special assignments, I found that every man who had any chance to get home and back was in the 50 percent. True, we had no official absences without leave that weekend, but some for whom I had stretched a point did not return on time. I felt badly put upon, especially as there was little that could be added to the discomfort that the maneuvers would provide for all, equally.

In contrast to the previous year, most of the 1942 maneuvers were done on foot, under a merciless sun that took a heavy toll in spite of the conditioning we had been through. On a day's march, the battalion would leave up to the equivalent of a company straggling along its track. Colonel Opie considered this disgraceful, which it was, and formed a provost guard under the regiment's toughest captain to follow along and boot stragglers back into line. The Bataan death march had come to light, and we were constantly reminded that the "Japs" would have less mercy than the provost guard had. All the booting and reminders of dire consequences in the world, however, cannot get a man doubled over with heat cramps back on his feet.

The maneuvers were run by umpires who used elaborate scoring systems to decide which side was performing most lethally. It was as good a training system as could be devised, but it was about as close to the war as a boys' game of tag is to a gang rumble. The naval battles of Coral Sea and Midway were fought in May and June; the Marines' assault on Guadalcanal was in preparation for August; in Russia, the German Sixth Army was battling toward its death at Stalingrad; in North Africa, the British had lost Tobruk and had turned at bay in El Alamein.

The maneuvers did show that the nation's production might was coming on to an awesome full stretch. We now had a full complement of vehicles and weapons, as well as the newly developed walkie-talkie radios and sound-powered telephones. Wood-burning cooking stoves had been replaced by gasoline-fired ranges, and the whoosh-clang sound made by the hand pump used to stoke up pressure in the ranges had replaced the sound of wood-chopping around the mess tent. One morning after a pleasant night's bivouac in a grove of tall pines, First Sergeant Robert W. Smith, bringing the morning report to be signed, was laughing about an exchange he had heard in passing a pup tent. The exchange was related to the long run of hot cakes we had been having for breakfast, and to the sound of the stove tender's pump:

First weary voice: "What-da you guess we'll get for breakfast?"

Second weary voice: "No need to guess — it's hot cakes. Can't you hear 'em pumping 'em up?"

Amazingly, an infantry company can chuckle through the dusty miles of a long, hot day on as little as that. Or on this earlier one, which I heard many times but cannot remember when or where it occurred: One of our files had the nickname Preacher. During a lunch break, the company was stretched out along the road and Preacher was sleeping. There arrived a delegation of ladies of the church from a nearby town, who were concerned about the spiritual welfare of this new young army. Their escorting officer brought them up to Tom Dallas, who was asked if there were religious leanings in the company. Tom was not one to overlook such an opportunity.

"Why, yes," he said, "we even have a man we call 'Preacher'."

The ladies were beaming approval of this when Preacher awoke and, not seeing them, announced loudly, "I'm so thirsty I wish one of you bastards would die so I could get your canteen."

Tom beamed proudly and the ladies departed, I know not in what state.

In the course of one of the week-long maneuver wars of that summer, I was reconnoitering by jeep for defensive positions. Each ridge line ahead appearing more advantageous, I went too far and found myself in the middle of the "enemy" advance guard — a company of the 1st Infantry Division. My driver and I spent two pleasant, lazy days as "prisoners of war" (POWs), and then peace broke out, and I returned to the company, which had no intention of relieving me of embarrassment.

"What kind of bird can't fly?" asked one (it may have been Preacher) loudly of the bivouac at large.

A chorus answered: "A jail bird."

This cheered everyone up, so I could not begrudge it.

In mid-August, the maneuvers came to an abrupt halt as the 29th was ordered to Camp Blanding, near Jacksonville, Florida. Again, the long truck convoys rolled, trailed by wives and sweethearts, leaving behind the sutlers with unsold wares and long faces. Blanding had just been vacated by the 1st Infantry Division, which, as it turned out, was on the way toward its November landing in North Africa. Mainly, we were interested in our own good fortune in being off the ground and into canvas-roofed hutments, with a large lake nearby for swimming. Detachments from the division were sent off in all directions on special assignment, and the rest of us concluded that we would spend the winter in Florida. Leave seemed so assured that I wrote home to expect me. Happiness, after all, could be found in the wartime army.

Then, all the rosy colors faded. Colonel Craighill, coming back from regimental headquarters, called the company commanders together and told us to prepare at once for overseas shipment, destination unknown. I believe that by the time I got back to the company area, the wives and sweethearts, who had established themselves around Blanding, were there and knew what was afoot. I was greatly exercised about security and shooed them away, but not successfully.

The days that followed were a blur of movement as directive followed directive — a number of them, of course, contradictory — about what to pack and crate and where and when. H Company's reason for being was eight heavy machine guns and six 81-mm mortars. Before the war, some of my heroes had worked in the factories around Martinsville at crating furniture; they were put to work crating weapons. Evidently there is a difference between crating a dining room table and packing up a heavy mortar, for the boxes broke open somewhere in transit and we lost them all.

In the midst of this preparation, an assortment of lieutenants, fresh from OCS, arrived to fill out the regiment's depleted complement of officers. H Company received three. Lieutenant Robert B. "Crow" Williamson and I had been the only officers with the company for the past four months and had run the platoons through the sergeants. They had done well and, I think, found it hard to give over. Lieutenants Vincent Labowicz, Fred Harvey, and Tom Murphy reported in on a pale yellow autumn morning, and I sat down with them to explain the barely organized confusion then in progress. Of the five of us, Williamson and Labowicz were to die on the beach; Harvey, Murphy, and I survived the war with hurts of varying degree.

Preparation continued — a lot of it doing and then undoing — and then, one bright, cool day in mid-September, we were convoyed to the Blanding railroad siding, loaded into long lines of passenger coaches, and started "north." The wives and sweethearts were successfully barred from the loading area, but, as it turned out, they knew more about "north" than we did, for they were waiting when we arrived at Camp Kilmer, New Jersey.

Kilmer was another raw new cantonment built as a port of embarkation for the European Theater. The 29th troops were the first of the hundreds of thousands that were to pass through its barren confines over the next three years to feed the insatiable demands of the European front. It was a booster pump in the personnel pipeline and not a place to win a soldier's affection.

The wives had penetrated the secret of where we were headed with apparent ease, but we still went through elaborate security motions. All identifying marks of the division and its regiments were obliterated and replaced by shipping code numbers. I do not recall exactly when mail censorship by company officers was begun, but it was probably at Kilmer; orders were not to indicate in letters that we were outward bound.

The new type of helmet was issued to replace the old soup-bowl model of World War I. Heavy weapons companies were issued 1903-model Springfield rifles to replace the .45 service automatics we had been carrying as individual weapons. The rifles must have been resting in their Cosmoline coating since 1918. All of one night was spent in cleaning them, and the next day was spent in cleaning up the Cosmoline that had been transferred to the barracks walls and floors.

Strange orders came down: Shoe polish was not to be carried, or coat hangers (fire danger was the reason given for the ban on shoe polish; no danger was cited from coat hangers). Company commanders had to inspect and certify the contents of the two barracks bags (A and B, naturally) in which each man was to carry a constantly changing list of items. At my inspection, one young soldier was obviously reluctant to dump the contents of his bag on the table. I told him to get on with it and out tumbled a pocket Bible, which he picked up in angry embarrassment and threw across the supply room. One of my regrets is that instead of just ordering him to pick it up, I had assured him that I was carrying a Bible.

In the midst of all this, the officers were assembled and told by Colonel Opie that he would not be taking us over; he had been promoted to brigadier and transferred to a new command. It was hard for me to imagine the regiment without him, for he had been in command from the day I joined. I had come several times under the cut of his disapproval and had not enjoyed it, but he was a gentleman and a soldier to admire and respect.

The wives' intelligence network was matched by that of the NCOs. I found out I had been promoted to captain when a delegation of sergeants came up and, with blank-faced indifference, handed me a set of double bars. Up until then, I had felt some leeway as a first lieutenant commanding a company; now I would do it as a captain, with no allowances to be expected. The bars weighed heavily. Later in the day, orders came down confirming the NCOs' prior word, which I would not again doubt.

Twenty-six September ended the excesses in preparation. We struggled onto troop trains at the Kilmer siding and, laden near to immobility, made the short trip to the ferry slips at Jersey City. Then, through a soft, black night and over the city-soiled waters, with the skyline of Manhattan looming in the background, we pulled alongside a pier where towered the huge, dimly lit shape of the *Queen Mary*. It was an eerie sight — files of souls struggling under heavy burdens through the cavernous pier-side warehouse toward a pool of light at the bottom of a gangplank. Charon may not have to check the passenger list for his crossings of the Styx, but we were identified by name and number for this embarkation into the unknown. One of my less sterling warriors tried to drop out of sight in the gloom; he was found behind a pile of baggage and booted back into place; no one was to miss the trip on this luxury liner.

Up the gangway the files toiled and then down into the depths of a weird, twilit world of multistacked bunks. Wedged in with its gear, the company had barely room to move except in unison. Officers fared little better; a dozen of us were shoehorned into double-tiered bunks in a richly paneled cabin originally designed for a privileged couple. Little of the night, or of energy, were left to contemplate the deeper meaning of all this, so I slept.

The next morning was gray and colder as the *Queen* slid down New York harbor and out into the Atlantic; thus, the United States projected toward war a shipload of what were presumably some of the best of its young manhood. Whatever our quality, many were soon afflicted with motion sickness, and, on a crowded troop ship, this is an illness all share by proximity.

For seven days the mighty *Queen* plowed its furrow in the sea in solitary splendor, first angling south so far that the ship's crew appeared in white shorts, while the passengers sweated in wool. When we turned north into damp cold, we could only hope that the German submarine command was as puzzled as to our destination as we were. A comforting report from an ever-elusive source had it that the *Queen* was too fast for convoy travel, and that changing course at calculated intervals made it impossible for a submarine to bring torpedo tubes to bear on her.

There must have been over five thousand on board, including most of the Stonewall Brigade; all seemed in constant motion, going to and from meals, work details, inspections, meetings, and the obviously useless drills for abandoning ship. Down on the troop decks, crap games ran nonstop. These — and carving names on the deck rails — were the extent of the recreation available. The meals were an introduction to a long spell of British wartime diet: watery, starchy, and largely tasteless. The troops ate standing and the officers sat down in shifts; travel on a wartime troop ship offends all the senses.

On the sixth day at sea, it became apparent that our destination was the British Isles. Several warships of the Royal Navy appeared low on the horizon, signal lamps blinking, to escort the *Queen* through dangerous waters. I was on the top deck, where the battalion's automatic rifle men had been stationed to supplement the ship's antiaircraft defenses, for we were in the Luftwaffe's as well as the U-boats' range. I was watching the questing warships through the gray haze when there was a bump and then a tremor underfoot, and a shout that we had run down one of the escorts. From the towering deck, I had not seen the low-lying warship — later identified as the *Curaçao* — that, for reasons never determined, had cut too close across the *Queen*'s bow. The *Curaçao* was cleaved in half and went down with all 332 hands. The *Queen* did not pause; later in the day, all officers were assembled in the huge, ornate lounge, and the ship's captain told us of the damage to the hull. He stressed that no word of this must be mentioned when we got ashore. He spoke calmly, though obviously under a great weight of responsibility. At the time, the *Queen* was probably as important to the war effort as any ship in the Allied fleets. So far as I know, the secret was held secure.

The next day, the crippled *Queen* dropped anchor in the Firth of Clyde, off the Scottish port of Greenock. We stumbled onto lighters and were ferried ashore, making what must have been a less than inspiring sight staggering along under the weight of rifles and baggage, so short of breath that no one muttered, "George III, we are here," as normally would have been done. Nevertheless, a British army band boomed and clanged; we heard for the first time an air raid siren wailing for real; barrage balloons with dangling cables designed to keep off low air attack swayed on the ends of their tethers in the damp and the smoke. Thus, the Stonewall Brigade arrived in the European Theater of Operations. It was to be a long stay.

With no hesitation for speeches or ceremony, we were herded into strange-looking side-door passenger cars, had time to note that the British freight cars and locomotives were about half the size of U.S. rail transport, and started rumbling south. The Luftwaffe having lost the air war over Britain had turned its attention to the Russian front, but targets were still not allowed to linger long at British ports.

All night, we clattered through a countryside of what seemed miniature fields and cottages. Occasionally, the train ground to a halt at station platforms, dimly lit by blackout lamps, where ladies in dark uniform poked trays of vaguely sweet buns and mugs of hot tea at us. By sight, sound, and taste, it was as though we had landed on a strange planet; to the British, it must have seemed that we were the alien creatures, lacking only olive drab antennae sprouting from our foreheads. Over the next two years, custom blunted but never entirely obliterated the habit of regarding each other askance. For some on both sides, there was instant and lasting dislike; for more on both sides, it was liking and respect; for quite a few, it was marriage (which possibly reflected some of both attitudes).

Britain, at this moment of its finest hour, was usually gray by day with rare interludes of sunshine. It was universally Stygian by night except for the weak, hooded lamps marking main road intersections, and for the slashing beams of antiaircraft searchlights across the skies. There was the overall shabbiness of three years of austerity in which every resource and effort had been bent to war. The debris of the Battle of Britain had been cleared from the streets, but buildings — except for air raid shelters and street-corner reservoirs of water for fire-fighting — were left in disrepair. The sounds of England's streets were hobnail boots on pavements, air raid sirens, ack-ack guns cracking, orchestras playing for the dances that seemed part of every night in every town. Its sights were uniforms; buildings agape and broken by bombs; traditional green fields; sunken lanes lined with ancient trees; thatched cottages; lines of people waiting patiently at bus stops, train stations, movie houses. Its taste was of Brussels sprouts, old mutton, Spam, powdered eggs, dehydrated potatoes, and strong tea. It felt damp, but its morale was unyielding. There was much about wartime Britain to admire; gradually, we fitted into it in one way or another. Our

23

abrasive presence was accepted by the British, sometimes, but not always, because we were a wartime necessity — like rationing.

Early the next afternoon, our train was switched off the main line and clanked to a stop on a dreary-looking siding. Across the tracks and a road was a large complex of red brick buildings: Tidworth Barracks on the Salisbury Plain. We tumbled out of the cars. Stiff from the long, cramped ride, we formed up and marched behind guides to the barracks. In its way, Tidworth was as dismal as Meade had been nearly two years before, but it was the disconsolate look of age, not raw newness. Its architecture dated from the Victorian height of empire and was built for the ages: brick, iron, slate, concrete, and asphalt, all constantly damp or drenched, for rain and mist dominated the weather on the Salisbury Plain.

H Company was assigned a two-story section of one of the red brick barracks. Each floor consisted of a long, cavernous room heated by a single fireplace. Lining the walls were double-deck bunks covered by stained sectional mattresses, called "biscuits" by the British army. The company began to long out loud for the "Meade Country Club."

Officers were quartered in an equally gloomy, gabled two-story building that bore that name of Lucknow, a British cavalry station in India. The 2d Battalion's five company commanders were packed into one room that in peacetime was probably the sitting room of a captain's suite. There was one toilet and a bath tub — dating to the turn of the century — on each floor. In front of the quarters were athletic fields of the thick green sod that plentiful moisture and underlying chalk produce.

As dour as the quarters were, we came to prefer them over marching and training in what seemed a continuous rain. The division went on a seven-day-a-week training schedule with forty-eight hours off each month for a regimental pass, en masse, to London. Such a schedule was bound to be monotonous and repetitious. Not all of our equipment had arrived; some of it, like our 81-mm mortars, had been lost and not yet replaced. Much time was spent in road marches, the standard one being a thirty-miler that at its halfway point circled the prehistoric monument of Stonehenge. I do not recall that much curiosity was expressed about the origin and purpose of those enormous slabs of bluestone, or how they had been transported and erected at a time so far back beyond the dawn of history. We were more

24

concerned with getting back the fifteen miles to Tidworth and out of the damp. We never encountered a tourist at Stonehenge, and rarely a car on the road. The British were fixed in purpose and place for the duration and moved about very little except on duty.

The trips by special train to London for the two days off each month had the supercharged aspect to be expected, given the pent up — not to put too fine a point to it — social and physical energies, and the unspent pay, of healthy young men. Some used their energy at the British Museum, and some burned it on a nonstop binge, but for most it was just a continuation of the lonely sense of being strangers in a strange land.

The ride back to Tidworth was dominated by the diehards of the binges, whose favorite protest against another twenty-eight straight days of drill was to pull the emergency cord that ran through the coaches, bringing the train to a shuddering halt. This disturbed me more at the time than it would now, for I was overly concerned with what impression we were making on the British. Their troops, I thought, had a smarter and fitter appearance; the crash of their hobnail boots and stomping, arm-swinging march style was in contrast to our simple, but no less precise, drill movements. As it turned out, in battle, their best was no better than ours, and their average on about the same level; these things had not changed much since 1776 and 1812.

Early on during the stay at Tidworth, I underwent a spell of lethargy that, unfortunately, coincided with the arrival of a new regimental commander who had an exceptionally keen eye for dawdling. The result was predictable. After two years of practically day in, day out pressurized routine, I had slacked off on inspections and let infractions slide. The company, most of whom had been bored with soldiering longer than I had, immediately reflected this: The colonel's first inspection turned up shaggy hair and spotted uniforms.

His name was Canham, Charles D. W. He was tall and thin to the point of being skeletal; professional by training and nature, he never slacked off. It took some time to find that he could be dryly affable and had a sense of humor. I never heard him laugh, but he could smile.

No affability or humor showed when I was summoned after the inspection. All I met was a cold, hard stare and a recital of my deficiencies. Even knowing I had it coming did not help my feelings. He characterized my performance as that of a "good file" — that is a good fellow — rather than a good commander. I was asked if I had anything to say. A quick inventory of mitigating circumstances showed bankruptcy, so I said that I did not cotton to excuses. This was barely true; it was just one of those responses made in the 116th by rote, sometimes loosely, and came easily to mind. It proved the best form of *mea culpa* in this case, as it does in most, for I found that while Colonel Canham would tolerate a mistake, if not repeated, he would not abide an excuse. He told me to get the company in shape, or he would put in a commander who could. This stung enough to get me back on the job; and the company had further reason to wish the war were over.

We marched away that winter of 1942–1943, and for recreation we played Americanized versions of rugby football and snooker pool, and learned the attractions of pubs. There were day and night training exercises. One attack exercise called for overhead machine gun fire using live ammunition. We put wooden stops under the gun barrels to be sure they would not be accidentally depressed, but just as the firing started an umpire came along and kicked down the stops, saying that they ruined the realism. This particular bow to realism has preyed on my mind ever since, for somehow a muzzle dropped and a burst of fire hit in among some riflemen, killing one. It was the 2d Battalion's first such death in training, but not the last; casualties rose as live ammunition and high explosives played a larger part in training to kill. Even with the vast quantities of ammunition used in training, however, I doubt that such deaths during the entire war matched those of a peacetime hunting season.

A British glider troop's training camp nearby appeared wasteful of life to the point of disregard; few days passed, it seemed, that a caisson bearing a flag-draped coffin, escorted by troopers in red berets, did not rumble by on the way to the British army cemetery.

In May of that year, 1943, the 29th Division was ordered from the Salisbury Plain to the extreme south of England. It was the start of the enormous concentration of troops and materiél for the invasion of the Continent, but we were not aware of this.

Most of the 150-mile march was made on foot. On fair days, this was like marching through a springtime garden, but there were also the usual downpours, chafed feet, and the difficulties of marching in long columns. Tempers exploded in simple declarative statements about the pace being set by runaway race horses, and then by lame turtles, and in any event by idiots. The same low mentality was attributed to those who selected bivouac sites. It was, all in all, a good, high-spirited march.

Instead of concentration in one area, as at Tidworth, the division was now scattered by battalions over Cornwall and Devon, the 2d's post being a small wartime British army camp outside the picture postcard village of Bridestowe on the edge of Dartmoor. The camp consisted of a collection of pre-fab huts. The village had a pub, a church, and a huddle of thatch-roofed cottages. Here we stayed over the next year training for the invasion of the Continent.

Training started off in a fumbling way, for there was only a vague idea as to what we were supposed to do. At first, it was all conducted on land, using homemade mock-ups of landing craft. Dartmoor was probably as good a land area for this as any, for it seemed afloat in rain. Its vast, rolling, pitching stretches of spongy turf were usually clouded in mist — a desolate, eerie, sometimes bleakly beautiful place. We came to know, but never to love, Dartmoor as we tramped across it, shivered in its cold winds, and slept on its liquid surface. On the first night there, I pitched my tent in a depression for protection from the wind, to awake in the early morning in a cold flood, as the hollow proved to be a runoff for rainwater. A night in Bridestowe Camp, out of the elements, came to be something to relish.

About two months after we had set up at Bridestowe, command of the 29th passed to the man who was to dominate it, and all in it, for the remainder of the war. Major General Charles W. Gerhardt entered the sphere of every command in the division from platoon on up, and with impact. Physically and by temperament, he conformed to General Philip Sheridan's specifications for a cavalryman, which he had been before the war: short, wiry, daring, and quick. Everything about him was explosive: speech, movements, temper. He dominated the division by knowing exactly what he wanted done, discarding those who failed to produce it, and rewarding those who did. As with all formulas for success, the key to this one lay in unrelenting application. His displeasure was applied to commanders, as the most effective pressure points, and our efforts to avoid it resulted in a divisionwide alacrity. His approval could be just as emphatic; naturally, both judgments were at times misplaced.

The general's first impression was apt to be final, and the odds were against redeeming an unfavorable one. With the good luck that was my main military asset, his first contact with H Company was on one of its better days, and he was approving. A few days later, he met the company again, this time on the road, swinging along smartly under its heavy load of machine guns and mortars, possibly because it was headed for camp and supper — or, in company usage, "Headed for the barn." Lieutenant Murphy, who was bringing it in, reported to the general and was complimented on the sharp appearance. So, I was off to a good start with this unusual soldier, but there was always the next encounter to consider. I would have felt easier had I realized then that he was as reluctant to revise a good opinion as a bad one.

I came to admire and respect him, for he sounded a certain trumpet in confusing and dreadful situations. Even so, I never felt comfortable in his presence; I suppose one never does with a strong and single-minded personality. It is my unsupported opinion that the number of divisional commanders of this caliber that the nation can muster in a given war is unfortunately fewer than the number of divisions of good soldiers that can be mustered. The combination of courage, professional ability, imagination, and ruthlessness found in these few is rare enough to make them beyond price in war. This is not to be construed as total praise of exceptional divisional commanders; their characters, overall, lie well within the human scale, including its lower ranges. Again, however, when a battle or a war hangs in the balance, there is no substitute for their particular attributes, whatever their defects.

At Bridestowe, with regimental headquarters miles away at Plymouth, the 2d Battalion became more than ever a closed-in world. Due deference was shown visiting senior commanders, but their underlings, arriving to inspect our efforts, were treated just well enough to avoid a charge of open hostility. All within the clan, however, was not harmony. Colonel Craighill had left from Tidworth to become regimental executive officer; his imprint on the battalion was such that his place would have been hard for anyone to fill. For the one so named, it was impossible. He was a good-natured man, small of stature, and he showed courage in the unresponsive atmosphere that developed after our brief try at adjustment did not come off. Then, at Bridestowe, he led the battalion astray on a couple of exercises and the verdict was in: The company commanders concluded that he was incompetent.

This opinion seethed for some time before we decided to provide Colonel Canham with it. This was a mistake, for we had overlooked that appearing as a group on such a mission violated any number of Articles of War — a fact pointed out in icy tones by the colonel. The five of us shriveled visibly as his reaction to our advice registered; self-preservation demanded a run for moral cover, so we stammered out that our own fates were of no importance; we were thinking of the battalion and by implication, the outcome of the war and the fate of the Republic. It was probably in spite of this lofty stance rather than because of it — and from his understanding of amateur soldiers — that the colonel admonished us to support our commander instead of undercutting him. He added that any further approach as a delegation to advise him on who should lead his battalion would result in the loss of our skins. We believed him.

On the way to Plymouth, riding in the rear of a weapons carrier truck, we had bellowed out some of the innumerable stanzas of "West Virginia's Finest Ham," led by Larry Madill of E Company, and "Bless Them All," the British army song we had adopted. The return to Bridestowe was somber with the consciousness of having performed a sorry act. Afterwards, we tried harder to support our commander, but he had handicaps that limited what the best will in the world could do for him. After an interval to ensure that we had learned our place, Colonel Canham replaced him with Tom Howie, by then a major; Major Sidney V. Bingham arrived and was assigned as his executive officer.

In the meantime, Captain George Boyd, the battalion adjutant and Headquarters Company commander, and I had been switched in our jobs, an exchange that may have represented the colonel's lingering memory of his first inspection. I cannot, however, complain of unfair treatment, for Boyd was a better heavy weapons man, and I turned out to be a pretty good adjutant. It was hard to leave H Company after three years at the heart of its trials and triumphs; it was where I had learned whatever I knew of being a soldier. I suddenly realized what I owed to these men and tried to express this at my last reveille formation. I do not believe it got across; reveille is not the most effective time to convey emotion to the foot soldier.

Thus, the clashing, meshing, and shifting of personalities went on at all levels in the tight little world in which we lived and labored. Relationships were regulated outwardly by rank; below this surface were rivalries, common purpose, sudden animosities, longer-lived loyalties, and an unfailing and redeeming resurgence of humor. All together, it amounted to that elusive, powerful force called comradeship that war seems to bring to its highest and most enduring level.

We welcomed Tom Howie with enthusiasm. As his adjutant, I found him to be as he had been when I first met him as a fledgling lieutenant at Fort Meade: considerate and unexcitable. He was the same at Saint-Lô and the end of his story. That, however, is a year away in the order of telling.

The summer of 1943 was hardly distinguishable from any other seasons on Dartmoor, except that the wind and damp were warmer. We continued beach assault training, gradually gaining direction and doctrine. Fortified areas, girdled with barbed wire and spotted with bunkers, were staked out for assault practice; even so, our efforts seemed unreal then, and even more so looking back on them now.

Marches took us past the eighteen-foot–high granite walls of Dartmoor Prison, where over a century before some five thousand Americans, captured in the War of 1812, had been held in disease and hunger. Time, as a stagehand, jumbles scenery and circumstances in a most unaccountable way.

So far, we had hardly been near water except for that falling so consistently from the sky; assault landing craft were still wooden mock-ups, and a ship's side was a building with a cargo net hung from the eaves. The mighty resources of the Allies, however, were being brought to bear on mounting the cross-Channel attack. A beach assault training center had been established at Woolacombe, on the northwest coast of England, and here the 116th moved that autumn to practice with the weapons and tactics that had been developed for breaching the Germans' Atlantic wall. We worked with a new type of flame thrower and heavy wire-cutters and formed plastic explosive into charges to be fixed on the ends of poles to push under barbed wire entanglements or stuffed into satchels to sling into bunkers. Drivers and mechanics practiced waterproofing vehicles and fitting the exhausts with snorkel devices for driving through surf. For the first time, we saw the amphibious trucks (DUKWs), and the highly secret tanks fitted with flotation devices designed to allow them to be off-loaded in deep Channel water from whence they would "swim" ashore.

The tactics were based on thirty-man boat teams — the capacity of the personnel landing craft — organized to fight independently against the complexes of bunkers and field fortifications in the landing areas. A typical boat team was made up of rifle and machine gun sections, and flame thrower, wire- cutting, and demolitions sections.

Much of this training was with live ammunition, and, inevitably, there were deaths and injury. I visited in hospital a particularly handsome H Company lad, sightless for life from a premature explosion of a demolitions charge. The experience shook me by its witness to the waste of war and all its parts, but I still could not envision the vaster waste of killing and maiming by deliberate effort, and not by accident.

The three weeks at Woolacombe wound up with battalion live-fire exercises, and then a dry run by the entire regiment, along with its supporting artillery, engineer, and tank units. The 2d Battalion's live-fire exercise went very well; we created a tremendous racket and much flame and smoke and were judged by the umpires to have devastated the frequently devastated bunker system that represented a sector of German beach defenses. We were in good spirits at mess that night. All was dank, as usual; the mess tent walls, the powdered eggs, potatoes, and even the fried Spam seemed to have a coating of water. But it was autumn, we were young and American, and our thoughts and conversation homed to football. This was Tom Howie's subject, he having been a star at the Citadel and coach at Staunton (Virginia) Military Academy. Down the years come the whining of the gasoline lantern, the harsh white light and stark black shadows it threw, the feel of the damp, and Tom Howie demonstrating a quarterback's moves through a series of plays. For the moment, we were transported from England's dripping shores and the importance of balanced firepower in a boat team, back to the United States and the importance of a quarterback's feints, handling a football. It was a pleasant respite.

Back at Bridestowe, drill practice continued; company teams played a rough round of touch football, Bob Hope's troupe put on a performance, and occasionally, when we were in camp on weekends, there were the vigorous parties that healthy young men with an awareness of approach to the precipice would have.

A more elaborate affair was a dance given at regimental headquarters in Plymouth, in honor of Viscountess Nancy Astor, born a Langhorne of Virginia. Because of her origins, this dynamic lady, then a member of the British House of Commons, treated the 116th with grace and favor, including correcting any Stonewaller whose uniform she considered not up to snuff. During the few steps of a dance I had with her, I dropped the names of a small number of prominent Virginians whom I knew as a newsman. She recognized none of them, and I drew only a cool, puzzled look. As I yielded to the next cut-in, I was aware of having made no impression on one of the most distinctive personalities of the time.

Early in December, an announcement arrived of a two-week course at the University of Oxford for Allied soldiers. Taking unabashed advantage of the adjutant's first look at incoming paper, I got Tom Howie's permission to attend. There followed two of the most pleasant weeks of the war. Balliol College, where the course was held, was as chill and damp as the rest of wartime England, but the lectures on the history, life, and arts of the isles were entirely enjoyable, and there were no examinations. The one discordant note was struck by a member of the class who stole one of the college's treasured ale tankards from the refectory. There was a tremendous outcry of indignation, and the tankard reappeared in its place.

I was back at Bridestowe by the holidays. "White Christmas" was again the favorite song. There were no packages from home because of the shipping that would have had to be diverted from carrying war materiél. The homesick note in letters rose to a higher pitch, and the New Year was seen in with as much of a bash as we could muster. We knew that 1944 would be the year of invasion, but we knew not where or when and had no idea at all of the cost.

Had we been analytical, we would have seen that 1943 had belonged to the Allies. The German Sixth Army had been frozen at Stalingrad, and the last major German offensive in Russia (at Kursk) had been defeated; Sicily had been secured and a hold established on the Italian mainland; the long, costly campaign to take Guadalcanal had been won; the air war had been carried to Germany.

Invasion exercises were under way again with the start of 1944. This time, the practice was at a coastal area called Slapton Sands, near Dartmouth. Individual boat team rehearsals continued, but the main events were large-scale, full-dress affairs. For one of these, we were teamed with the 16th Regiment, 1st Infantry Division, to give the mock-up area another of its regular poundings. Considerable effort was being made to establish rapport between the foot soldier and the airman, so, on this exercise, a number of fighter-bomber pilots went along for orientation on how we operated. I think the principal result was to convince them that the air war was less uncomfortable, if not less deadly. At the end of the day of slogging through sand and brush, they departed without a backward glance. We may have gone a little overboard on our demonstration.

The divisional commander never let up on our own orientation. One tactic he used was to appear at a position established after an assault exercise, demanding of the commander — company or battalion — how long it would take him to get his outfit assembled, march to another point two or three miles away, and redeploy. If the commander's time estimate was considered excessive, he was judged lacking in energy and organization; if too brief, he was considered lacking in judgment. In either case, he was ordered to execute the move; great activity ensued, contributing to the strained look that commanders habitually wore at the time.

The toll from working with lethal materiél continued to mount. On one wind-whipped day in early spring, I was standing on a dune above a section of beach that was being cleared of British anti-invasion mines so that we could use it for practice landings — it being obvious by then that the Germans were not in a position to invade. I saw one of our Ammunition and Pioneer Platoon approach an uncovered mine and for some reason touch its top with the toe of his boot. There was a blinding flash and a clap of sound, and he disappeared as by a magician's sleight of hand. The illusion terminated in pieces of anatomy plopping into the sand around us.

The incidence of psychological casualties also began to mount. Low-back pains and other disabilities, apparently long endured, now became acute and their claimants departed,

From this weeding out, and from unremitting work, the battalion became tougher by the day. The divisional commander's list of both proscribed and required actions grew: No smoking in vehicles; no more than a cup of leftover food in a company's garbage cans after a meal; helmet strap always worn buckled on the point of the chin; always sixty yards between vehicles; each officer and NCO to carry a notebook and pencil to record orders. Everyone in the division was required to know, verbatim, the general's version of the correct alignment of the sights in aiming, and the sequence in squeezing the trigger. "Top of the front sight in center of the peep sight, bull's eye resting on top of the front sight": These words are fixed in memory, as is the correct trigger squeeze — "This with the second joint, finger well through the trigger guard, and thumb alongside the stock."

The general's visits to the battalion followed a pattern, any part of which could cause extreme discomfort. He would arrive without notice and immediately challenge any and all to marksmanship with the .45 service automatic. Eccles Scott, commanding officer (CO) of G Company, our best shot, was the only one in the battalion to beat him. The general paid off the ten-shilling bet, but it was plain he did not like to lose. After marksmanship, he would make a tour of the training, firing questions as he strode about to see that his many edicts were followed. Any training that he judged to be complicated drew a blast; he demanded simplicity in tactics, a lot of yelling, and much shooting. The divisions's battle cry, which he originated — "29 Let's Go!" — was a required shout in everything we did. To overcome a reluctance to shoot after so many years of emphasis on safety, he directed officers to fire at fence posts and trees when riding along roads and lanes. I never did this without cringing at the possibility of a ricochet into an animal or a house; three years of obsession with safety in handling firearms was hard to overcome. It was one of the general's wiser edicts.

Privates, and NCOs to some extent, did not look on his visits with misgivings, for the word had gotten around that he did not hold them accountable for mistakes. Not so with officers; even the brashest drew mental blanks before a cold, unwavering stare, a volley of questions, and the knowledge that there was no recourse if answers were hesitant or wrong.

It was inevitable that Tom Howie would run afoul of this arbitrary, demanding man, for Tom was neither. He drew fire on some minor matters, and then for a battalion truck mishap — a cardinal offense about which he had to report to the general in person. One evening just before retreat, the general bounded into battalion headquarters obviously ready to lay about him. Tom reported and received a barrage of critical observations and questions, including the standard ones about the correct sight picture and trigger squeeze. Tom made a mistake, and the general delivered the verdict that he had undoubtedly already decided upon: He relieved Tom from command on the spot. This was not unusual at any level in the pressure-cooker atmosphere before the invasion. I had seen officers flattened by it, but in this instance, the flattening did not take place; the scene that the general had dominated up to that point became all Tom Howie's. On the instant, he seemed to grow to a presence that filled the room. With immense dignity, he asked if that was all. The general, who had remained his normal size, absent-mindedly replied, yes, that was all, and turned and left without another word.

An account of war is altogether a human account. This particular encounter of the major general and the major stands out in my memory. The general — a proud, imperious man — was not imperceptive. I believe he never forgot that moment when the quiet major towered morally over him; he had intimations that here was stronger stuff than he had thought. No more than six months later, the general saw to it that the major's name dominated in death the blood-red scene of Saint-Lô.

Tom Howie was assigned to regimental headquarters as plans and operations officer (S-3). Major Bingham was named to command the 2d Battalion, the first and only West Point commander we were to have. He was unorthodox and irreverent enough to lead the free spirits of citizens turned temporary soldiers, and there was nothing stuffy about a battalion under his command. I found him interesting and comfortable to serve, though an accumulation of small irritants could trigger a formidable explosion. In the clutch, he could be as tough and unyielding as any and held the battalion together through some dire straits. He won the Distinguished Service Cross (DSC) on the D-day beachhead; later, in Normandy, he was wounded, evacuated, and returned to command the regiment. After the war, he was a charter organizer of the Special Forces.

The tempo of preparation was constantly stepped up as winter wore itself out in frigid bluster. The final drafts of new officers and men arrived to top the battalion off at full strength. Where previous replacements had been mostly in their mid-twenties, these new ones were younger; an aging global war now in final and full career was requiring the country to dig ever deeper into its manpower.

There were more full-dress rehearsals at Slapton Sands. Again and again, we loaded onto landing craft that pitched and rolled out into the Channel and then roared landward to drop ramps over which we lumbered to flounder through surf to the beach and go through the assault drills. So often repeated, these drills became a ritual dance performed by fire, flame thrower, and demolitions teams deploying, then advancing, in stylized movements, to blast paths through barbed wire, throw flame through the firing apertures of bunkers, and blast them with explosives. Battalion and regimental staffs entered on cue to direct further movements. Unfortunately, D-day weather and German guns were to provide a tune different from the one we had practiced on Slapton Sands and throw the ritualized movements into discord and near chaos.

There were also practice loadings on the USS *Thomas Jefferson*, a prewar passenger liner that was to convey us across the Channel to the offshore area from which we would be launched in landing craft for the beach. To foot soldiers, the *Jefferson* was an unreal world of comfort and of food that came near to matching our exaggerated memories of a world before the war.

Another sign that the 29th had been assigned a critical role in the invasion was the unusual interest shown by the high command. British General Bernard L. Montgomery, who was to command the overall assault, spoke one day to a multitude of the Blue and Gray gathered around his jeep in a huge meadow. I was too far away to hear, and all I could make out was a small figure standing and gesticulating from the hood of a jeep. As he concluded, there was applause and also some Bronx cheers, as might be expected. On another occasion, we were addressed by General Omar Bradley, who was to command the U.S. Army forces. He assured us that casualties would not be as heavy as forecast. Few, I believe, really contemplated being a casualty at all, and so considered this assurance aimed at others. General Dwight Eisenhower also inspected the division, but I did not see him.

All in all, something of a pre–big game atmosphere developed in which we, as an enormous first team of thousands, were fussed over, exhorted, and anxiously examined as to competence and spirit. On only nine Allied divisions (six infantry, three airborne), and the supporting engineers and armor in the initial assault, would rest not only a large share of the Allied fortunes, but also the fortunes and place in history of those in authority over us. I hope that they did not give to the latter prospect as much thought as to the former, but they were, after all, human.

On the whole, I do not believe that individuals in the invasion force were greatly worried, for we were caught up in the complex mechanics of the mission and our separate tasks in it. Training and discipline had molded outlook and response. I do not recall any questioning of a frontal assault on prepared defenses from the unstable base of the English Channel. Word had come through of the bloody nature of beach assaults in the Pacific, at Dieppe, and at Salerno. There were, too, the tales a number of us had grown up on of the World War I frontal offensives that had bled so profusely a generation of Western manhood.

Some comforting divergences could be found between our prospects and these bloody examples. The size of the Pacific islands had allowed little surprise as to where the attacks would be made, while the long, convoluted western coast of Europe offered opportunities for deception as to the exact place we would hit. The Germans were laboring frantically to make their seacoast fortifications the equivalent of those that had taken such a heavy toll on the western front a quarter-century before. They had now, however, a new flank to consider: Into the space over their heads, the Allies could put a preponderance of warplanes, and launch airborne and glider troops. Then, there was the difference that, in 1944, the German army was fighting for its life along the vast eastern front. How the cross-Channel attack would have fared without this particular advantage, I do not care to contemplate; certainly, without it, the attack could not have been undertaken in the way it was. We did not, in any event, question the plan or doubt our ability to execute it. No force of such size has ever trained longer or more intensively for a single mission, or with resources more abundant and their delivery better organized.

While the rough winds were still "shaking the darling buds of May," the final concentration of the assault force began. The Stonewall Brigade assembled at Blandford, a large British army installation in Dorsetshire. The 2d Battalion gave Bridestowe Camp a final raking and brushing, turned all excess toilet articles over to a nearby orphanage — soap was a scarce and valued item in wartime Britain — and left the moors. Watching the trucks pass out the camp gate, I was impressed that the battalion was at its peak, as ready as an outfit could be. Its people, many of whom I knew by name, looked hard and fit; trucks, weapons carriers, and jeeps, in dull olive drab, were spotless — and moved at careful sixty-yard intervals. I was not aware of it, but we were never to look exactly that way again. Battle turned sleekness to a wary, worn look; after D-day, the companies became a kaleidoscope of changing faces.

We closed into crowded Blandford on 19 May. The days there were rare ones of some sun and warmth that helped dry Dartmoor's dampness from bones and bedrolls. While the concentration continued, there was some lull in duties, and in the evenings Jim Bagley, the long and lanky transportation officer from Alabama, and I found rides into Bournemouth for what we called pre–D-day rest and recreation. This Channel-side resort had been a regimental watering hole for the past two years, and we had found a welcome in the large home of an English dowager who could organize parties on short notice. These eve-of-D-day parties bore no resemblance to the Duchess of Richmond's grand ball before Waterloo, but we were not troubled by historical comparison. The invasion was not mentioned, though obviously it was at hand: The south of England had been sealed off from the rest of the country; troops were everywhere (more than one-and-a-half million of them); every leaf-roofed lane was packed with vehicles and supply dumps; the air was charged with the vitality and power of all this restrained violence, primed and ready to detonate.

Parties at Bournemouth ended as the battalion was shifted from Blandford to the marshaling area for O Force (units for the Omaha Beach assault) near the embarkation points at Poole and Portland. Here, we were quartered in tent camps, called "sausages," set up in every patch of woodland. The camps were operated by service of supply (SOS) units, our host being an ordnance battalion. It is axiomatic that no outfit is ever satisfied with how another runs things, so there was an immediate complaint about our host's operation of the kitchens, their output being compared to the hardware that ordnance serviced. (Soldiers' figures of speech tend toward vivid comparisons; men detailed to haul away latrine buckets were "assigned to cooks' and bakers' school.") The feeding complaint reached a climax when the ordnance people closed some of the kitchens in preparation for an inspection. This made the already long mess lines intolerable and triggered Major Bingham's wrath, which proved more formidable than the inspection; the kitchens were reopened.

It did not take a man assigned to an infantry battalion long to discover that his job was different from those of the rest of the army — that he lived harder and was likely to die sooner. There was always griping, but also some pride over this unequal burden of the war effort. Now, as the true nature of the D-day assault became apparent, we realized fully that no matter the volume of supplies accumulated, or the brilliance of the planning, the job would finally come down upon our shoulders. When this was proved out, we became convinced that no one else was really in the war, except, perhaps, tankers (shielded by steel plate) and combat engineers who cleared beach obstacles, and repaired roads and bridges under fire. The division's 121st Combat Engineer Battalion was redoubtable. With this realization, foot-soldier arrogance reached a level that must have been thoroughly obnoxious to the rest of the army. It was also of considerable moral support in doing a job that needed all the moral backing possible; the Combat Infantryman Badge became one of the most prized pieces of decorative metal of the war.

Shortly after our arrival, the marshaling area was sealed off, and no one was allowed in or out except by pass. Then the operational briefings started, and we learned details of the plans that had been so many months in the making for launching what General Eisenhower termed a "great crusade to liberate Europe."

Captain Sherman Burroughs, operations officer (S-3), and Lieutenant Bob Hargrove, intelligence officer (S-2), brought down the D-day order, which we pounced on as though it were a second Book of Revelation, scanning first the mission of the regiment and then coming into sharp focus on the details of the 2d Battalion's job.

Here it was, on smudged mimeographed sheets, and in staff college–taught format, with headings, subheadings, sub-subheadings, and references to annexes, stating that we would assault the Easy Green, Dog Red, and Dog White subsectors of a stretch of beach dubbed Omaha. Our three rifle companies would go in abreast, preceded by three companies of the 743d Tank Battalion. Directly behind the rifle companies would come the Combat Engineers to clear and mark lanes through the beach obstacles for later arrivals; then the craft bearing H Company's heavy weapons, the battalion headquarters, and three batteries of antiaircraft guns were to arrive.

All of this was to follow a split-second schedule (the rifle company boat teams were to touch down one minute after the tanks). Within thirty minutes, the first four waves, including all of the battalion, were to be ashore. To our right, the 1st Battalion was to attack on a one-company front; two battalions of Rangers were attached to the regiment with the missions of assaulting the Pointe de la Percée and Pointe du Hoe promontories extending into the Channel, which intelligence said were manned by heavy coastal defense guns. Two companies of the secret tanks, fitted with flotation "skirts," were to swim in from over three miles out to lead in our right flank company and the lead company of the 1st Battalion. Over the next three hours, wave was to follow wave at five-, ten-, and thirty-minute intervals until all of the Stonewall Brigade, its supporting artillery, more engineers, medics, and antiaircraft guns, naval parties, and amphibious truck companies were ashore. I looked no further into the innumerable waves of other units that were to follow to build up and expand the beachhead.

It is unlikely that even under the most favorable maneuvers conditions such a schedule could have been followed. Disruption is the stuff of battle — it can make a deadly type of nonsense of any plan; it did so in this one.

The 1st Infantry Division was to command the initial assault on Omaha, and we were attached to it for that phase. Attacking on our left would be the 16th Regiment of the 1st Division. The Stonewall Brigade's principal objectives were two roads that angle up from the beach to the crest of the bordering line of cliffs. These exit roads were essential for moving heavy equipment from the beach. The right-hand one, looking from the Channel, led to Vierville, the village at its top (prosaic planners called it Beach Exit D-1), and was to be taken by the 1st Battalion. The 2d Battalion was to secure the left-hand one (Exit D-3), leading up from the beach to the village of Les Moulins.

The intelligence annex spelled out the difficulties: In order to reach the beach, four separate bands of obstacles, ranked between the low- and high-tide marks, would have to be navigated. These ranged from logs, angled into the sand, with mines attached to their tips to explode if struck by a landing craft, to steel gatelike structures and giant jackstraws of angle iron. The Germans understood the importance of the beach exit roads as well as we did and had them blocked with concrete bunkers, barbed wire, and mines. The tops of the bluffs were zig-zagged with fire trenches.

It was estimated that between eight hundred and one thousand troops manned the Omaha sector defenses, and that of these a large proportion were Poles or Russians who had defected to the Nazis; their willingness to fight to the death for the Third Reich was considered dubious. The closest German counterattack force was believed to be a first-class infantry division stationed around Saint-Lô, about twenty miles inland. War is, ultimately, chance — which adds another dimension of madness — and this division with all its artillery was not twenty miles away on D-day; it was deployed in and close behind Omaha Beach. In fact, it had been there for three months, undetected by one of the most intensive intelligence operations every conducted.

To oppose all this and destroy it, the Allied command had assembled a blasting, shredding, and tearing force of awesome proportions: From midnight to dawn of D-day, heavy bombers were to saturate all known targets; preceding H-hour, the beach fortifications were to receive a half-hour of air and naval bombardment — one object of the air attack being to crater the beach with ready-made foxholes for the assaulting infantry. The guns of two battleships, three cruisers, and eight destroyers were to lay heavily against the defenses of the Vierville and Les Moulins exit roads. Large landing craft had been fitted with banks of rockets to be launched from close inshore, just before the assault teams touched down; all artillery pieces and tanks were to fire from their landing craft as they approached shore, and the tanks going ashore directly preceding the infantry were to finish off any remaining opposition by direct fire.

In bare recital, the Omaha Beach defenses were impregnable; the weight of our attack, overwhelming. On balance, we believed the odds favored the overwhelming, somehow overlooking that the weather could cast the deciding lot, as it very nearly did. Wind, high-running seas, and low-hanging clouds blanked out the air attack on the beach defenses, swamped nearly all the tanks and artillery, ran most of the assault teams astray, and left many of the defenders untouched. The attack had to be put bloodily back together again in the chaos on the beach, under the cover of smoke from unintended brush fires; the defenders' souls did prove conquerable, but at a considerable price.

All of this, however, lay in the future. In the meantime, we moved in the heady world of preparation and expectation of success. Some of our young greyhounds maintained that they were going to race across the beach and up the bluffs so fast that if they hit any barbed wire they might spring right back into the Channel. Sherm Burroughs, always a steady and cheerful presence, vowed to keep up his boat team's spirits by reciting the "Shooting of Dan McGrew" all the way in, timing the last line with the falling of the ramp.

So, basking in innocence, we went about the final days. Each boat team was minutely briefed on its objective, including a session with a plaster terrain model. The last pieces of equipment arrived, and each man assembled his personal combat load. The first effort to shoulder these loads showed them to be disastrously overweight. Some Stonewallers from southwest Virginia registered this by loping and braying about the camp under their packs, saying that as long as they were loaded like jackasses they might as well sound like them. Discipline in the Stonewall Brigade was hard, but it never kept the soldier from expressing his opinion when things became too foolish. Invariably, it was a mistake not to listen and heed.

The British infantry had a saying that it was always ordered to attack uphill and at the junction of two or more map sheets. I would say that it is the U.S. Army's proclivity to oversupply itself and to put too much of this surplus on the backs of its infantry, a practice that added to its many burdens in Vietnam. In any event, the Stonewaller of 1861–1865 would never have been able to fight his fierce battles carrying the load his namesake struggled under on D-day. There is a pang of pity and regret looking back down the years to the man under that burden: a special canvas assault jacket with large pockets front and back in which were grenades, rations, mess gear, raincoat, a Syrette of morphine, toilet articles, motion sickness pills, water purification tablets, DDT dusting powder, a paste to put on boots in case he encountered chemically contaminated areas, a small block of TNT for the quick blasting of a foxhole (of all the disturbing sounds I heard on Omaha Beach, there were none identifiable as from those blocks of TNT), and two hundred francs in a special currency issued by the Allied Military Government in order that trade could start with the Normans as soon as he was ashore. Around his waist was strapped an ammunition and equipment belt from which swung an entrenching tool, another first aid packet, and a canteen. From his neck hung a special assault gas mask and extra bandoliers of ammunition. In addition, each man carried his individual weapon, and, if a member of a machine gun, mortar, flame-thrower, or demolitions team, his part of that load.

All of this was put on over a new wool uniform that had been impregnated with a chemical to neutralize blister gases that the Germans might employ. These uniforms felt constantly damp and gave off a sour odor that, it was predicted, the Germans would be able to smell from the time we left England, and that might trigger a gas counterattack.

All of this excess burden, provided in the name of concern for our welfare, was borne with ribald humor, along with complaint. We had come to feel that we could do anything, and there was a great enterprise at hand in which to prove it. I recall only two troublesome notes during those last days of innocence. One was a letter from regimental headquarters, directing me to explain why an unauthorized machine gun was mounted on a halftrack that was to tow in one of my company's 37-mm antitank guns. Such departures from the ordained were not taken lightly in the 116th. From habit, I started composing a reply based generally upon the machine gun's having followed my lads home from our host ordnance battalion. Then, struck by the ridiculous aspect of having to explain one gun on a day that was to be dominated by thousands of guns, I threw the letter away. Months, and a number of battles, later, another directive came down, requesting that I explain my failure to answer the first one. This turned out to be the then–regimental adjutant's little joke, which I did not catch until after having expressed, over the field telephone, my opinion of his grasp of reality.

The second matter was more serious. The evening before we were to leave the marshaling area for embarkation, I returned to camp from some mission to find one of my men isolated under guard. Major Bingham told me that he had refused to obey an order and was under arrest. I was told to straighten it out in short order, for there was no time for such foolishness. I knew the man as a quiet, hardworking soldier. This action was so out of character that I did not descend on him with the usual references to a court martial and other dire consequences. This is not to say that I showed wise, fatherly benevolence, for I was not that wise and certainly not benevolent when it came to refusing orders. I did, however, try to find out the reason, and this was not easy for he was not articulate. As we talked, it dawned that his rebellion was not really against what he termed "being pushed around," but against all the lives, effort, and materiél being projected across the English Channel to destroy lives, effort, and materiél arrayed on its other side. Perhaps I caught his feeling about this because—while never doubting that it had to be done—I had a similar sense of its insanity. There was no rational explanation to give him; I could point out only that he had a particular job that he knew how to do well and that at this late date no replacement was possible. He seemed relieved at having gotten his feelings across and said that he did not want to let his squad down and would like to go back and do his best. I was happy to have the problem resolved and felt as a priest perhaps might on having struck the right note at confession.

I do not know how many of the D-day force were similarly carried forward to their separate fates by duty, loyalty, and pride — to acts that violated every rational fiber of their being — but I suspect the percentage was high. It was not until much later that I realized a soldier exists in war on two emotional levels: On one level, he kills and destroys; the other level, carefully insulated from the first, is his rational self, lying dormant until it can with some safety reassert itself. It is a self-induced schizophrenia, essential to emotional survival. In a world gone insane, it is only good sense to be as happily insane as one can be.

Schizophrenic or not, the next day, 3 June, we shouldered the heavy invasion loads and departed the marshaling camp for embarkation. If our ordnance hosts cheered, it was for the departure of troublesome guests, and not for heroes leaving on a crusade. Another tenant outfit moved in right behind us, and I am sure the hosts wished again that they could get back to their military hardware and out of housekeeping for foot soldiers.

The ride to the port was short. We stumbled out of the trucks, again shouldered the top-heavy loads, and filed down a dockside street, lined with Victorian structures, and onto lighters to be ferried out to the *Thomas Jefferson*, and for the last time clambered up cargo nets to the deck. Again, no bands played; no girls waved handkerchiefs while struggling to choke back tears. The closest to a send-off to war was a leathery old English dockworker who croaked, "Have a good go at it, mates." It was like loading for a Slapton Sands exercise except for the pounds of equipment we carried. The accommodations were spacious for a troop ship, and I noted for the first time that the oppressive crowding, so much a part of army life, thins out markedly the closer the approach to battle. The initial assault on the two beaches — Omaha and Utah — assigned to the U.S. forces was to be made by no more than three thousand of all the hundreds of thousands of troops then crowded into southern England.

The weather was of that "un-rare" English June that threatens both fair and foul, ready to go either way. The harbor was jammed with craft of all the sizes and shapes that had been developed for landing tanks, troops, and cargo on beaches. A heavy concentration of barrage balloons ringed the harbor, tugging at their tethers, for the Luftwaffe was still feared. There had been, in fact, a German air raid on the marshaling area a few nights before. Although light and brief, it had inspired such foxhole digging that Sherm Burroughs had gravely presented his private award, which he called the APO (Army Post Office) Box with Key, to those of the staff who had dug the deepest and fastest. I believe I was a recipient.

Having stowed their packs, the Stonewallers lined the deck rails to look with tolerant curiosity over the scurrying launches and blinking signal lamps. The activity was, after all, for the sole purpose of getting us onto the coast of Normandy; in such a manner, actors may regard stagehands.

Since leaving Bridestowe and being confined to camps, the battalion had lost some of its physical edge. There had been daily sessions of calisthenics, but there is no substitute for marching, running, and field work to keep a soldier fit and sharp. To look sharp would have been hard enough under any circumstance in those sour-smelling uniforms.

H-hour was set for dawn of 5 June. We spent the first night on the *Jefferson* quietly, and also the next day, unaware that the convoys with the longest routes to travel, already at sea, had been turned back at the last moment as worsening weather led to the hard decision to delay for one day. The weight of such a determination is unimaginable by anyone who did not have to make it.

No agonizing choices had to be made on the *Jefferson.* We were under the control of "the plan," and, until it was knocked awry by nature and the enemy, we would follow its dictates. The delay was taken in stride in the relative comfort of the *Jefferson,* though it was an added ordeal to those on the cramped smaller vessels of the armada. We continued to enjoy navy food, and the boat teams rehearsed yet again the drill of moving from quarters to loading stations on deck where the assault craft were swung, like lifeboats, from davits. So passed 4 June.

The next day, word came that the assault was to go in with the dawn and the low tide of 6 June. Ships' signal lamps set up a frenzy of blinking; that afternoon, the antisubmarine net across the harbor curved open, and the *Jefferson* churned out into the wind-roughened waters of the Channel. Vessels of all shapes and sizes, towing barrage balloons as if in some gigantic, colorless carnival procession, were before, behind, and to either side — part of the fleet of some five thousand then streaming out in long columns from southern England. My view of this mightiest of all armadas was limited by the overcast, and my interest in it was narrowed to bringing in the battalion command post at its designated point near the Les Moulins beach exit, exactly thirty minutes behind the first wave; then to following the assault to the top of the bluffs and on inland beyond the village, Vierville, the battalion's D-day objective. All this was to be done within three hours, after which we would dig in and await further orders for destruction of the German army, little of which could by then be left. I had selected on the map the location of the command post outside Vierville and had, in all confidence, advised regiment where it would be. Like other pat plans for Omaha Beach, this one did not last the first moments of landing, and it departed unfulfilled and fully forgotten.

The last dinner on the *Jefferson* was quieter than usual, and there was no special talk of the morrow. Afterwards, our Chaplain Charles D. Reed held a religious service above the throb of the ship's engine and some milling about by those on last-minute missions. The chaplain was a quiet and serious man who had joined us at Bridestowe. He stayed the war, working hard at spiritual leadership and steering clear of our transgressions, over which I expect he sorrowed and prayed. Some, of course, jibed at him, but he made no reply and went his earnest way. There were probably more than the usual number of private prayers launched that night as the realization grew that this was not another exercise, and that at dawn metal would be flying both ways. Friends gravitated together; I noted no bravado, or even the normal crap game. An engineer officer played an accordion, but there was no singing. Some of us talked with a British navy frogman who, several times, had gone in on Omaha Beach from a submarine to examine its rows of obstacles. He could tell us little that we did not already know from study of the terrain model and aerial photographs, but it was curious to talk with a man who had already trod with apparent ease the stretch of sand we were making such a titanic effort to reach.

Reveille was to be at 0200 with assault craft loading an hour later. The prospect did not lull anyone to sleep, but most went to their bunks early. Another sign of the uncrowded way to battle was that I had a cabin to myself. I prayed, as always, but do not recall just how my petition was couched; it was probably rather personalized. Then, I lay on a bunk in that strangely lonely cabin and leafed through a *Collier's* magazine given me by Bob Jones, a friend from Murfreesboro whom I had found to be an ensign on the *Jefferson*. The magazine was full of war pieces — all to the effect of how well everything was going — that I found vapid, as wartime writing tends to be, so I put it down and tried to sleep. I was not aware of any dread; perhaps it was lack of imagination, or just curiosity about the trial of the drills we had practiced so long. I dozed, but was awake when the ship's gongs sounded reveille.

The engines had quieted; we were in the transport area twelve miles off the beach; even the big liner was registering the waves. I put on the uncomfortable uniform, boots, and leggings and then shaved for D-day. Breakfast in the ornately decorated salon was unreal: bacon and eggs on the edge of eternity. Perhaps every breakfast — and every moment for that matter — can be so considered, but a D-day breakfast has its own special bizarre quality. We were quiet; each withdrawn into some private inner place; conversation was perfunctory and absent-minded. Everything moved automatically, except for a brief discussion with the ship's mess officer about whether troops going into battle should first clean up after breakfast. Cleanliness of his mess decks must have been the crux of the war so far as he was concerned. The troops settled this by simple going back to their quarters to start shouldering their loads, certain that the crusade in Europe would not be delayed to call them back for KP (kitchen police). At some point, a message from General Eisenhower was read over the address system; a traditional ritual of unequal historical results, the effect depending more upon the emotional state of troops than on the eloquence of the commander.

Back in my cabin, I struggled into my own gear, featherweight compared to a rifleman's, but heavy and awkward enough. The final item was a life belt: two brown tubes of rubberized material to be inflated by triggering capsules of carbon dioxide. So, clad for the crusade, I wedged out into the line of laden officers crowding down the corridor toward boat stations. There were handshaking and exchanges of good luck, routine enough, but having this day a dreamlike, "outward bound" quality. We filed out through heavy blackout curtains into the dark of D-day; a cold, damp wind was sweeping the deck and fairly whistling through the rigging. The *Jefferson*'s rise and fall in the uneasy water was more noticeable here than it had been below. As eyes adjusted, I found the darkness was not complete; one of the requirements for the airborne assault was a late-rising full moon, and now some faint light from it penetrated the overcast.

Some three hours before, around midnight, eighteen thousand paratroopers in three airborne divisions, two U.S. and one British-Canadian, had dropped to secure the flanks of the invasion area. While we were loading into assault boats, the German command was gradually awakening to the fact that the war was being brought to Normandy.

My boat team assembled on station. We counted off and then helped each other into the open-topped, rectangular steel box that we were to ride to battle. It had a motor and rudder at one end and a hinged ramp at the other; on a platform above the motor, the figure of the coxswain, hunchbacked in a bulky life vest, was dimly visible. It then occurred to me that this was the first time I had seen him; I had no idea how well he knew his job or, equally important, how determined he was to get us ashore at the right place. On the day we loaded, I had noted what was apparently the first briefing of the coxswains on the mission. This seemed a rather casual link in the carefully forged chain of preparation. Now, it was too late for more than regret over things done or left undone.

We sorted ourselves out to long-rehearsed places in the cramped, swaying confines of the landing craft. Some continued an awful seasickness already under way, while others started being sick — a burden I was spared and did not fully appreciate until years later when I underwent a spell on an ocean crossing.

A stream of cryptic orders flowed from our ship's address system, and ships' crews checked from craft to craft; from a control launch in the darkness of the Channel came unintelligible words amplified through a bullhorn. We in the boat were in something of the position of a patient on the operating table listening to a surgical team discuss his condition in strange jargon; in this case, the operating table was swaying wildly. It all meant something, for suddenly, with a rattle of chains and screech of wire cable, the craft began to move slowly down the *Jefferson*'s side. It was met by a rising swell that slacked the cables and then dropped us with a crash as it rolled on. The next move down brought us fully into the waves. By some miracle, we were not slammed into the ship's side; the propeller caught, and we followed a shepherding launch out to join other craft, circling as in some strange conga line in the dark, with red and green riding lights appearing on the crests and disappearing in the troughs of waves that were four and five feet high.

Everyone in the heavily laden, low-riding craft was soaked by blowing spume before we hit the Channel. It seemed that we would surely swamp, and I passed the word to inflate the life belts. Not only our persons, but reels of telephone wire, radios, and demolition packs were girded with these belts in the hope that, if lost in the surf, they would float ashore. The sudden expansion of perhaps seventy-five belts added to the bulk already crowding the craft, and so we rode, packed like sardines in an open can, feet awash in bilge water and altogether uncomfortable. My position was by the ramp so as to lead off with the infantry "follow me" bit, and it seemed that we were slamming into waves with enough impact to start any rivet ever set.

After about an hour of circling, the control launch passed a signal, and the assault craft carrying the second wave of the Stonewall Brigade peeled off into line astern and began battering through heavy seas toward Normandy; thirty minutes ahead of us was the first wave; twenty minutes behind would come the third. For more of us than we yet realized, it was a wild death ride going in with the tide.

2

Omaha Beach

I think I went into that action [First Manassas] with less trepidation than into any subsequent one. Inexperience doubtless had much to do with it, and discipline told on me from first to last.

Captain Randolph Barton, CSA
Stonewall Brigade (1861–1865)

For the next two hours, the line of assault craft pitched and rolled toward Normandy and a gradually lighter horizon as we closed with the dawn of 6 June. In my boat, there was no conversation. Talk would have been difficult in any event above the roar of the engine, the wind, slamming of the waves against the ramp, and the laboring of the bilge pump that just managed to keep up with the water washing in over bow and sides. We simply stood packed together, encased in equipment, inarticulate with the noise and with the enormity toward which we were laboring. I recall offering no prayers and having no particular worries other than whether we were coming in on Dog Red sector.

The line roared past the great, gray shape of a battleship, either the *Texas* or the *Arkansas,* that was to have by then obliterated the Les Moulins defenses. The ship's huge guns were silent because of the near disaster, unknown to us, developing on the beach. The naval fire-control party that had accompanied the first wave had been blacked out by the curtain of German fire that had descended along the waterline of Omaha Beach, and nothing was known of what was happening beyond that curtain. We bored on toward it still unaware that it existed. It was now within half an hour of scheduled touchdown at 0700 and as fully daylight as the overcast allowed. Signs that things were going amiss abounded, had I been battle-wise enough to read them: those silent guns of the battleship, indicating that it was out of touch with the assault and fearful of firing into it; a trickle, instead of stream, of return traffic from the landing of the first wave, which told of craft either destroyed or landed badly off target. Still another ill omen was the vacant sky where we had expected to see fighter-bombers diving and strafing the beach. We were unaware that the clouds had obscured the beach and moved the air bombardment inland beyond our sight and hearing.

A haze of smoke, barely darker than the dull morning, was the first sign of the shore, and then the line of bluffs that lay behind the beach began to loom above the Channel waters. Finally, it was all dimly visible, just about the time that our craft shuddered to a halt on a sandbar two hundred or so yards offshore. We were in among the beach obstacles: big, ugly structures of iron or logs partially covered by the rising tide. The coxswain failed on a couple of attempts to buck over the bar and then dropped the ramp. This may have been fortunate for us as well as prudent for the coxswain, for had the landing been made closer in, we would probably have attracted the attention of still largely intact defenders and drawn some of the machine gun, artillery, and mortar fire that was knocking the first wave apart. As it was, the German gunners had too many tempting targets closer at hand to bother with our more distant one.

So, as yet physically untouched by the battle, and in automatic response to the dropped ramp, we lumbered off in three files — center, right, left — into the cold, shoulder-deep surf. The life belt under my arms lifted me to the crest of an on-rolling wave, and here, flailing around to keep right side up against a top-heavy load, I caught my first full glimpse of combat, the inner sanctum of war toward which we had struggled so long and painfully. The sight was not inspiring or reassuring: Where Channel and shore met was an undulating line of dark objects. Some of the larger ones, recognizable as tanks and landing craft, were erupting black smoke. Higher up the beach was a line of smaller dots, straight as though drawn with a ruler, for they were aligned along a sea wall. Scattered black specks were detaching themselves from the surf and laboring toward this line. Looming up between beach and bluff, through the smoke and mist, was a two- or three-story house. Such a structure was a landmark of the Dog Red sector, but I could not see the road that angled up from the beach to Les Moulins. I believed that we had come in on target, but I ceased worrying greatly over whether we had or not. There is a definite calming effect to the casting of the die, and the die had been irrevocably cast on Omaha Beach.

The wave passed on, and in the trough I touched bottom, to be lifted moments later and carried again toward France. Such was the pattern of my advance in the greatest amphibious assault of history: up wave and down trough, propelled forward by a powerful, in-sweeping tide, regardless of any lessening fervor to open the second front in Europe.

The invasion had allied itself with gravity, and there was no discharge from it for either the paratroopers of the airborne assault or for we who came by sea. Our voluntary act was to step out of landing craft and out of aircraft. From then on, gravity — as its tides — pulled us into battle. This alliance with natural force was not entirely harmonious. The tide's sweep was not directly inshore but tended strongly eastward and carried much of the 2d Battalion far off its long-rehearsed objectives. Indifferent gravity had also brought paratroopers down wherever aircraft commanders dropped them, and this turned out to be in many unplanned places. All in all, the balance of natural force on D-day was conceded to the enemy; fortunately, he took only limited advantage of it.

The effect of alternate lift and fall with the waves was to gain views of the battle that were like the stopped frames of a motion picture. From the crests, the beach was visible, and then, in the troughs, only the green-black water of the passed wave. Thus early in combat, I developed what was to be a lasting regard for surface depressions. Omaha Beach, coming into clearer focus, made the successive walls of water between me and its exploding horror more and more anticipated. This high regard for wave troughs was to transfer after a few hours in Normandy to the roadside ditch, which I continue to look upon as the most helpful of the foot soldier's few ready-made assets.

The thirty members of the battalion headquarters landing team, lifting and settling with the waves around me, like swimmers unaccountably wearing steel helmets, were still quiet and dumb with the sights that were unfolding. Dirty red splashes of shell bursts were walking regularly with rapid, short steps among the objects along the waterline. Off to the left, a solitary landing craft, freed of its load, skittered over the waves back out to sea, a sailor at its 50-caliber machine gun arching tracers in the direction of Europe. Much farther down to the left, a rocket ship loosed banks of missiles in gushes of white smoke. These missiles, I learned later, fell far short of the beach and did nothing more than further roil the already rough Channel. Overhead to the right, a single flight of the twin-tailed P-38 fighter-bombers streaked inland, and, close at hand, a solitary destroyer plowed along parallel to the shore.

None of this was audible to us. The wind, like the tide, was in movement toward France and carried the din of invasion inland. The scene was strangely vacant of the vast work that had been imposed upon it. I had imagined a line of warships and a sky crowded with planes supporting our assault. As the single destroyer and the P-38s melted into the gloom, this image faded, and with it the illusion that this would be largely another training exercise. The warships and planes were there as promised — the warships back over the horizon and the planes far inland — all masked by uncertainty and the weather. Had I known this, I would probably have considered it a poor excuse.

On the first day of battle, the foot soldier probes new emotional depths, and the findings, I believe, are fairly universal. One is a conviction that he is abandoned, alone, and uncared-for in the world. I looked briefly into this particular abyss on seeing our landing craft depart, and the nearly empty sea and sky. The thought came that the crusade in Europe had been called off as a bad job, and that we waterlogged few were left to struggle alone in the great, dark seascape. The first assault wave, already on the beach, did not resemble a battle line as much as it did heaps of refuse, deposited there to burn and smolder unattended.

Abandoned or not, the tide and our own exertions brought us in through the staggered lines of iron and log obstructions to where the surf was breaking and rolling up the beach. There was no evidence that the engineers who had accompanied the first wave had succeeded in blasting paths through the obstacles that now formed a barrier behind us.

The water was waist-deep, and we were moving faster. I would judge the time to have been about 0730, when the first shots directed, however impersonally, at our demise keened above the rale of wind and surf. A few yards to the left and rear a high cry, in hurt and surprise, shrilled "I'm hit!"

I looked around. The white face, staring eyes, and open mouth of the first soldier I witnessed struck in battle remains with me. The image of no one — loved, admired, or disliked — remains more vivid. His name I have lost; I recall only that he had been assigned a few months before in the building up of the battalion for D-day. My first words on the opening of the second front in Europe were not an exhortation of "forward and remember the regiment," but a useless shout to attend the wounded man. I do not know his fate, but I think he was gone before the medic reached him.

With the burst of fire, we all submerged neck-deep in the sea, for Omaha Beach was obviously not a place to stand up and be counted. I lay flat out, supporting my head above water by resting hands on the shifting sands, and gave attention to the fact that a few more surges of the surf and we would all be ejected onto the beach, strewn with many dead things, both man and machine.

It was now apparent that we were coming ashore in one of the carefully registered killing zones of German machine guns and mortars. The havoc they had wrought was all around in an incredible chaos — bodies, weapons, boxes of demolitions, flame throwers, reels of telephone wire, and personal equipment from socks to toilet articles. Hundreds of the brown life belts were washing to and fro, writhing and twisting like brown sea slugs. The waves broke around the disabled tanks, bulldozers, and beached landing craft that were thick here in front of the heavily defended exit road.

From this prone position at the water's edge, the beach rose above me, steep and barren. There was a wide stretch of sand, being narrowed by the minute by the tide, then a sharply rising shingle bank of small, smooth stones that ended at the sea wall. Against the wall were soldiers of the first assault teams. Some were scooping out shelters; a number were stretched out in the loose attitude of the wounded; others had the ultimate stillness of death; but most were just sitting with backs against the wall. No warlike moves were apparent.

From such a low vantage point, only the upper portion of the house could be seen above the shingle, its brick walls and mansard roof agape with shell holes. The top of the bluff was visible, but I could not make out the beach exit road. We had, however, come in not far off our appointed place. There were luckier sites to have landed, but also unluckier ones. On the whole, I have no complaint about fortune in war. In fact, should the nation ever strike a medal for those who have great good luck in combat above and beyond their deserts, I shall make unabashed claim to it.

While I was straining to see above the debris and still stay in the dubious protection of the water, one of the explosions that were rippling up and down the beach erupted close by; there was a jar to the side of my face, and blood started streaming off my chin. I do not recall any particular emotion on being thus blooded for the first time in battle, but I did realize that this killing zone was no place to linger. Those in defilade along the shingle embankment seemed in much better case. The members of my boat team had completely disappeared among the debris; I saw nothing alive to either right or left. Having decided that survival, never mind valor, lay forward, I tried to rise and found that I seemed to be hoisting the English Channel with me. The assault jacket's large storage pockets, the gas mask case, boots, leggings, and uniform were all holding gallons of water. My overriding doubt on the edge of Omaha Beach was not about success of the invasion, but over whether I would ever make it up the steep rise for twenty to thirty yards with my burden. I had long preached the army's hopeful maxim that a good soldier never abandons his equipment, but, without a second thought, I jettisoned the assault jacket into the litter in the surf and, free of its weight, went lumbering up the beach, streaming water at every step.

I reached the embankment gasping for air and retching salt water. Around me were familiar faces from a jumble of boat teams from F, G, H, and Headquarters companies. Those who had arrived with me were in about my condition. Others had been there longer and were recovering from the rough passage. All were quiet. There was no evidence of panic; the attitude, in retrospect, was that of soldiers lacking means and direction. The lee of the embankment was in the eye of the storm, and no one was inclined to leave it without some compelling reason, such as a better place to go.

Minutes later, a tall, very composed colonel dropped down beside me and said calmly that we must all work toward getting the assault started inland. My work at the moment was for breath and against nausea, and I must not have looked very promising as a source of dynamic leadership. In any event, he departed, walking upright down the embankment. I have no idea who he was, or of what became of him. Incredibly enough — and this may be a trick that memory has played — I recall his uniform as dry and clean, while the rest of us were sopped and sand-encrusted.

Gradually, my lungs and stomach stopped heaving, and, taking thought that this was, after all, a battle in which I had responsibilities, I took my pistol from its holster and from the plastic bag that was to have protected it from the water. The plastic had not availed, and the pistol was sticky with salt and gritty with sand. The slide, when I pulled it back to load a round into the chamber, stuck halfway. Up and down the embankment were lying M-1 rifles, Browning automatics, and light machine guns, all similarly fouled. Except for one tank that was blasting away from the sand toward the Les Moulins exit road, the crusade in Europe at this point was, for all practical purposes, disarmed and naked before its enemies. The Germans lost Omaha Beach for the lack of a single company of riflemen to descend and sweep us up. But, looking down onto our obviously helpless condition, they still stuck to their observation bunkers and gun emplacements. We may have sensed that this was all they would do. On no other basis can I account for the fact that I had no feeling of defeat and saw none exhibited around me.

At about this time, Major Bingham came over the embankment with some half-dozen soldiers in tow. He had been trying to get up the bluff at this point but was balked by weapons that would not function. His first words, "This is a debacle," delivered in his volley fashion, have remained with me, possibly because "debacle" suited the scene as well as any one word could. I can appreciate now the weight of responsibility for an immobilized battalion with an objective that was impossible to attain. He did not seem to be brooding about it. He told me to sort out the boat teams and round up some firepower, and then he left on the run down the embankment to look for a way up the bluffs.

In battle, I have seen a soldier on one occasion of crisis develop a whirlwind of activity, and on another become inert and bemused. Whatever the emotional quirks that give such opposite results, I was now caught up in the one that expresses itself in activity.

The battalion command post was my job, and, as a first step, I launched into a hectic effort to organize it. Communication was the first requirement — we were an army of radios and telephones, perhaps too much so. A sand-coated reel of field telephone wire had somehow arrived nearby, and I thought to run a line down in the wake of Major Bingham, but no telephone could be found. A few men of the H Company mortar platoon were along the embankment, but all we could round up was one mortar tube without base plate or ammunition.

German fire seemed now to have shifted to other areas. I left the embankment and ran down behind a tank-dozer that had been blown over at the water's edge. From here, the face of the bluff and the Les Moulins exit road were visible. From the volume of fire, I expected at this close range to see flashes and smoke from German guns. Not a flash was visible, and the only smoke was from burning underbrush on the slopes in two separate areas several hundred yards to the right and to the left. It was these common brush fires, set off by the shelling, that were the salvation of the assault on Omaha Beach. Under their screen, a few brave souls were already getting across the beach flat and up the bluffs. Whatever else was accomplished by the naval cannonade that preceded H-hour, nothing could have exceeded the value of those brush fires that it started inadvertently. In fact, they demonstrated that a few smoke shells would have served us better than all the weight of high explosive.

I continued splashing down the waterline, around and over the debris, in the direction the battalion commander had taken, and dodging from behind one stranded piece of heavy equipment to another. On one of these dashes came a second blooding. This time, I did not hear the explosion or see the flash, but there was another jar to the side of the face — opposite to the first one — and again I started leaking blood. With this incentive, I departed the dead awash along the waterline and rejoined the living at the embankment. My injuries, though much less serious than most at Les Moulins, were spectacularly visible. Two soldiers advised me I had been hit and guided me to an aid station set up against the sea wall a short distance farther down the bank. The aid station was the most purposeful activity on the beach; there was a multitude of casualties.

An aid man looked over the wounds on either side of my face and announced with professional authority that here was a rare case of a shot having gone clearly through one cheek and out the other without damage to teeth or tongue. Most of those around the station were 2d Battalion men who knew me, and they seemed to look on this wound as extraordinary, on a day when wounds were much in style. Whether it was because of a disinclination to void this distraction in a trying moment, or because it did not seem very important under the circumstances, I failed to deny the diagnosis and so abetted one of the minor tales of Omaha Beach: that of the captain shot through the face while his mouth was wide open, suffering nothing more lasting than dimples in the process.

The story turned out to be harder to bear than the wounds. It gained wide currency through Ernie Pyle, the war's best-known correspondent, who was on the beach later in the day and heard about the "miracle" wound, which he reported. I suffered this unmerited fame for a number of years but finally became fed up with it and started giving the accurate version, which my friends seemed reluctant to accept. A more immediate regret for not having quashed it came at the end of the war, when the order in which we returned home was based on a point system to which each Purple Heart contributed. I was credited with only one Purple Heart from D-day, having passed up a second one for the brief interest of those around me. The odds against wounds occurring in just this manner must be high, but that is as close as they come to a miracle.

The aid man sprinkled sulfanilamide powder on my face and made out a linen-backed casualty tag, which I have as a memento of D-day.

Having an excuse to do so, I sat for a minute looking at two large infantry landing craft burning near the shore and wondered what to do next. Eccles Scott, G Company commander, came by with part of his boat team in wake. He told me that they had landed far off target to the east and were trying to get back to their assault objective. I told him what little I knew of the situation. He and I were the only two of the battalion's five company commanders to survive the day on our feet: one was killed; two were seriously wounded.

I moved on farther down the shingle bank to the left, or eastward, and came to a stretch vacant of men and quiet except for the wind, waves, and beach birds that were swooping and crying. Omaha Beach was generally of this pattern: violent swirls of death and destruction with areas of quiet in between. It was as if the deadly funnels of multiple tornados were touching down at spots along the Norman coast, whirling men and materiél into broken pieces, and moving on to touch again.

I had come into the area about a thousand yards east of Les Moulins, where smoky brush fires had swept up the bluffs and screened one of the first penetrations. The face of the bluffs was blackened, but the flames were largely burned out and little smoke lingered. I could see American uniforms moving slowly near the top. A barbed-wire entanglement between the shingle and a beach road had been blasted open at this point, but machine gun fire from a distance, ricocheting off the road, discouraged trying to get through it, and I ran farther to the left to a bigger gap blown through the wire. Beyond this gap and across the flat, a smaller party of soldiers was starting in single file up the slope. I reached them without drawing a shot and found that they were from our 3d Battalion, which had landed by good fortune in this smoke-covered area.

The trail, traced through the ash and soot, zig-zagged between small, round personnel mines with which the slope was sown. It came out onto a plateau of green fields, bounded by the embankments of earth and brush called hedgerows. There was no indication, on this first encounter, of the life and death role that their passive presence was to play over the next weeks. Here, they were not defended, the Germans being concentrated along the bluff line. But soon, pushing inland, we would encounter German reserves building up around the penetration, using the hedgerows as ready-made fieldworks, and their deadly potential would become shockingly apparent.

Directly across the path at the top of the bluffs lay the first German soldier I had seen in two hours of battle. He was lying face down, very dead, a stocky figure in complete uniform from boots to helmet. I recall no particular emotion on stepping over the corpse; in the brief course of that morning, dead bodies had become commonplace; this one differed only in uniform and in title — "enemy." Nor did I, at the time, consider that this solitary, inert figure represented a small, visible success for our vast effort

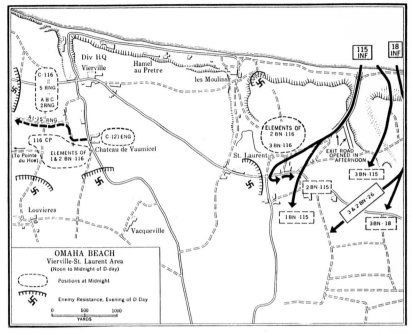

The widely scattered positions of the 116th's Battalions at midnight of D-day. The remnants of the 2d Battalion Headquarters were in the area shown outside of Saint Laurent. Courtesy of the National Archives, Washington, D.C.

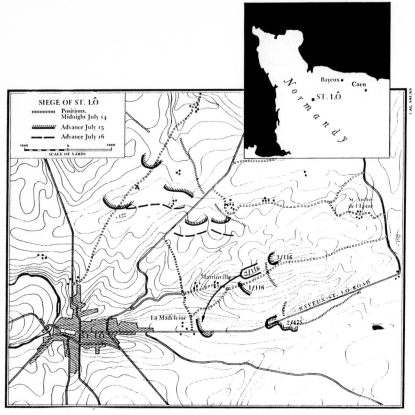

Five weeks after assaulting Omaha Beach, the 2d Battalion of the 116th Regiment (Stonewall Brigade) spearheaded the crucial attack on Saint-Lô. The battalion (designated 2/116) reached the Bayeux–Saint-Lô road but then was cut off from its supporting elements, the 1st and 3d Battalions of the 116th and the 2d Battalion of the 175th Regiment. Hills 122 and 192 played important roles in the battle, comparable to one of the Round Tops and to Culp's hills at Gettysburg, a much earlier battle in which the Stonewall Brigade fought. Courtesy of *American Heritage: The Magazine of History.*

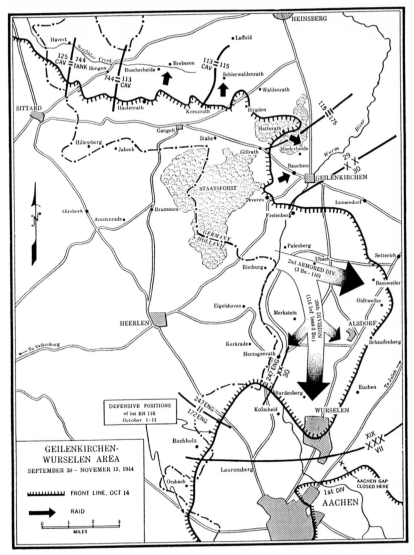

The 116th's penetration of the German front into the built-up area of Würselen. Courtesy of the National Archives, Washington, D.C.

at instigating death. The sheer monetary cost of reducing this one man to clay was tremendous. Even though the toll from our effort mounted, the per death cost must have remained high.

The time was about 0930. I had spent two unproductive hours on the beach. Ahead, small groups were moving inland, single file, along a hedgerow. I had to decide whether to return to the beach and bring up more of the battalion along this route, or to find Major Bingham to see if this was what he wanted. How much a disinclination to leave the present quiet for the chaos below influenced me, I do not know. The requirements of our long-rehearsed plan must still have weighed heavily, for getting to the objective seemed most important.

I had found this way off the beach largely by chance, but being a thousand yards from our appointed place, in the middle of another battalion, and in what I suspected was another regiment's sector, made me feel I had failed the test of battle, and the question as to what to do next seemed tremendous. Such rigidity was overcome before the close of that day. I became rapidly an advocate of taking whatever route developed as possible and least deadly. The foot soldier who survives in combat long enough — that is to say, a few hours — learns that plans and circumstances seldom coincide. Our plan did not provide for four- to five-foot waves, winds up to eighteen knots, or for an additional German division in the defenses. The results of these unforeseen factors were shock, inertia, and disorder; the only salvation of the day was the initiative and enterprise of a relative few who rose above the wreckage of the plan. Although they are for the most part unknown, the Republic owes them a considerable debt.

I was following in the path of some of these few, and I was not at all the happy warrior. Presumably a leader, I was leading no one, and following a faint war trace toward where I knew not, but certainly not where I was supposed to be. Luck, however, continued with me. I came out onto a lane and here caught up with the enterprising Major Bingham, who had with him some mixed sections of F and G boat teams, and a few men of the battalion headquarters. The lane led to Saint-Laurent, but from the east instead of from the western and southern route that we were to clear. We were indeed in the 1st Division's sector and mingled with elements of our own 3d Battalion.

Because, perhaps, of the spectacular appearance of my face, I was not taken to task for showing up alone. Major Bingham told me to bring up whatever elements of the battalion I could find, as he was to try for Les Moulins and our objective from this direction. It had already been determined that this route, too, was strongly defended. I washed the salt and sand from my automatic and its ammunition in a farmyard trough and then began a search through the shallow beachhead for men of the 2d Battalion.

And here it is that retrospect encounters gaps in continuity and detail that the most diligent search cannot close. Perhaps by this time, my capacity for registering separate sights and sounds had become saturated. Whatever the reason, the afternoon and night of D-day are a tapestry in which scenes emerge from a generally gray background and then fade or run together, or change position until it is difficult to fix them in time and place.

The course of the invasion has been reconstructed by painstaking research, hour by hour, thrust by counterthrust. Mine is an account of one soldier's groping through the fog of battle that lay so heavily over that day, and that still conceals parts of it. To try to make this search appear systematic and well-reasoned would be entirely false. It was haphazard and followed no logical pattern; I was aware only of what was occurring immediately around me, and I moved in a constricted compartment of sight, sound, and emotion.

I returned to the beach by the way I had left it. The burned-over area was still quiet, but, toward the Les Moulins exit road, the noise still mounted, and a far-distant rumble could be heard echoing from the Vierville exit road sector far down to the west. The source of the noise, however, was shifting from the German guns to our own. Destroyers cruising close inshore were methodically blasting the Les Moulins road and the face of the bluffs; a few surviving tanks were maneuvering in the limited space on the beach, adding the banshee screech of their high-velocity guns.

The lighter debris of the battle was stretched in enormous piles along the high-water mark, and the now-receding tide was leaving windrows of it over the exposed sand. The sea wall and shingle embankment were still lined with men, most of them wounded; others were emotionally broken beyond use. I was not the only seeker for able bodies. Officers and NCOs from the various engineer outfits were trying to organize men and materiél for clearing landing craft routes through the beach obstacles exposed by the receding tide. The fighters and workers were few; the abject watchers, many.

The aid station where I had stopped was still in operation and was a collecting point of disastrous information on the killed and wounded, some of it wrong, much of it sadly correct. Sherman Burroughs was gone, as was Lieutenant "Crow" Williamson of H Company, and Captain Madill of E (Madill had died far down the beach from this point; bad news travels fast in battle); Captain Boyd of H Company had been badly wounded, as had Captain Bill Callahan of F. As far as anyone knew, many others had simply disappeared into the maw of the Les Moulins exit road. The toll seemed all encompassing. The next day, I learned that sections of F, G, and H companies had climbed the bluffs, under the smokescreen of the brush fires, in the area west of Les Moulins. There, they had joined a surviving part of the 1st Battalion and the regimental command group near Vierville. This was only about a mile by road west of the 2d Battalion's fragments outside Saint-Laurent, but the mile was German-occupied.

Instead of being assembled on its objective, the battalion was stretched in a giant letter U, with the points inland at Saint-Laurent and at Vierville, the curved base running along the shingle embankment on the beach. It was a letter traced by a shaky and uncertain hand — thin, wavering, and with numerous gaps.

A few functioning soldiers came back with me to where the advance was stalled outside Saint-Laurent. My search then turned eastward through the beachhead, looking for sections of E Company reported to have landed far down in the 16th Infantry area. I met Lieutenant Boyle, the battalion supply officer, on a road back of the bluffs, along which were clusters of modest holiday cottages. On this day of history, we found three soldiers busily ransacking the poor contents of a cottage. We sent them on, but I am sure it was only a brief interruption to a career of looting.

Farther along this road we crossed a long, straight mound of dirt that looked as though it had been burrowed by a mole with a purposeful sense of direction. It was, in fact, a covered trench leading inland from the defenses on the bluffs. Some 2d Battalion men were in a cluster pondering the passage and what to do about it: hunt for explosives to blow it up or try to smoke it out. Major Bingham's need seemed more urgent, so they were pointed in his direction and the tunnel left to others.

Continuing, I encountered my first liberated Norman: an elderly farmer in a faded blue smock and black beret agitatedly pacing in front of a small farm cottage. My high school version of French did not seem to reassure him that the battle had moved on, so I proffered some soggy notes of invasion currency as more universally soothing. This, too, had no effect, possibly because it did not resemble any currency he had ever seen. We left him still pacing. So far, I had met one dead German and one disturbed Frenchman; neither, I would judge, favored the crusade in Europe.

None of this search through the beachhead was done leisurely, but at a half run, canvassing groups of antiaircraft men without weapons, signal men without signal equipment, and medics with waterlogged aid kits. None were from the 2d Battalion and none were armed effectively enough to be worth impressing into our ranks.

For some reason, Boyle and I went separate ways, and next I recall standing beside a small, rural hotel and the bodies of three Americans who had met final appointments there. The corporal of a live squad of the 16th Regiment deployed around the hotel told me that the dead had been there when he had arrived; he did not know their outfit. When I inquired if he had seen any units of the 116th, the corporal assumed that look of the soldier who is asked a question to which he does not have to know the answer; it involves a trace of piety and also questions the sanity of the asker. The ability to achieve this look was acquired in that war early in basic training; it is probably still practiced.

In tones matching his expression, he inquired of the squad, "Any of you seen anything of the — what was it, sir? — 116th?" They all assumed the same look.

"We ain't seen them," he summarized.

In the meantime, a lanky private had started firing at, and missing, the insulators on a utility pole. Everyone ducked, and, to the corporal's profane question, he said that these might be telephone lines that German observers were using. The corporal said simply that if he did not stop, he would shoot him.

64

They helped me arrange the lifeless young bodies in more decent postures along the shoulder of the road and cover their faces. I then continued in a search that, in retrospect, became more and more without pattern.

The Book of Joshua, 10:12, recounts that the Lord made the sun stand still at Joshua's request so there would be light to complete his victory over the Amorites. Not having Joshua's influence, the invasion planners instituted double daylight saving time to provide for a longer day of battle. Sometime early in that longer lit evening, I arrived at a crossing of lanes and realized that after many turnings I was thoroughly lost. Around me were only green fields and hedgerows; of war there was no evidence.

The sodden mass that had been a map had been long ago discarded. I turned, by chance and without much study, back toward Saint-Laurent instead of toward the encompassing German positions and out of the war. By that time, I was well into the sector of the 16th Infantry. There were boat teams of E Company probably within shouting distance of where I had turned back, but they might as well have been on another continent.

Back toward Saint-Laurent, I crossed a new road that the engineers had opened from the beach. Trucks, jeeps, ambulances, and weapons carriers jammed this outlet and were turning into the fields on either side. The Germans, west of Saint-Laurent, were still an effective stopper, but the pressure of men and materiél was building up in the beachhead. More helpful to the cause at the moment than these thin-skinned vehicles were three or four guns of a decimated armored field artillery battalion that had gone into position. Their red and white aiming stakes standing out against the green field are a remembered splash of color for no reason that I can determine.

In the stream of men and materiél flowing in from the beach in that relatively quiet sector east of Saint-Laurent was a unit of the 115th Infantry from Maryland, a sister regiment in the 29th Division. The day had not killed all regimental rivalry, for I recall passing it with the superior feeling of a combat veteran of several hours' seniority. The Stonewall Brigade had already seen the elephant; we knew its terrible aspect.

Near the straggling stone houses of Saint-Laurent, I came upon a post of our 3d Battalion that was surprisingly knowledgeable of the situation. I was advised not to go into the village, which had been shelled a short time before either by our warships or by German artillery; to those killed by the shelling, the source was probably immaterial. The 2d Battalion was believed to be to the right along a farm road to Les Moulins. This proved correct on a day of much misinformation. I found a sad remnant of the battalion, about ninety men, deployed around farm buildings facing German positions on high ground between us and the objective we had believed we would long since have occupied. Major Bingham was in a barn across a cobblestone-paved yard from the farmhouse. I told him that aside from the few men retrieved from the beach, I had found nothing except the dead, wounded, and emotionally crippled. He exhibited no dismay; such news must have been usual by then. There was no working radio or telephone equipment in the barn. But there was much coming and going of officers and runners as commands tried to locate units and issue orders for the next day.

Word continued to come in of death and disaster. The 111th Field Artillery Battalion, the long-time fire-support teammate of our regiment, had lost all of its howitzers in the Channel, and its commander was dead on the beach. Colonel Canham and some of his staff were inland near Vierville; he was wounded, his supply officer dead, and his adjutant seriously wounded. Parts of our G and H companies had also gotten over the bluffs in the smoke of the fires west of Vierville and were with the regimental command post. There was a vague report that A Company of our 1st Battalion had lost all of its officers and most of its men on the sands in front of the Vierville beach exit road. This later proved all too nearly true. Many of the fragmented reports of that night are now verified by names on monuments and memorial plaques across the country. On the memorial in Bedford, Virginia, the original home of A Company, there are twenty names under the date of 6 June 1944.

All in all, midnight found the Stonewall Brigade far- and thinly flung and hard-used. First reports set losses at about one thousand killed, wounded, or missing. The 2d Battalion had lost over half its ranks. This figure was scaled down, but not greatly, as some of the missing were gathered in. It had been as costly a day in the regiment's history as Chancellorsville and the death wound of Old Stonewall himself.

Of all the capacities that the years diminish, none leaves a greater void than the loss of the youthful ability for friendships without the questioning and restraints that complicate those of later life. I feel this void now in looking back upon friends gone on that 6 June. Together we had been through months and years of wartime confusions and strains; marched countless tedious miles; lived in mud and dust, heat and cold. I knew their problems both duty and personal, and they knew mine; the battalion and its business occupied very nearly all our time and thoughts, and it did not matter what else we might have or not have in common. Then, it all came down to this brief first day of battle on the coast of Normandy, and, for so many of them, it all ended. For the rest of us, what has been since has not been the same.

Sorrow was a presence in the command post that night, but it was still a dim presence. Weariness was there also, for twenty-four hours of intense physical and emotional strain had elapsed since reveille on the *Jefferson,* but neither weariness nor sorrow was dominant. Overriding both was what I can identify only as life forced to a hard, bright flame to survive. Experiencing this intensified life force, I believe, makes the acts of battle bearable and burnishes its memory. Soldiers who have experienced this surge have tried to describe it, and at the same time express the dread that accompanies it. Dread and exhilaration from the same source at the same time are emotions difficult to reconcile, and too confusing to construe.

There were few moments of battle that I did not actively dread, yet I experienced this surge and saw it in many around me. Under its influence, men were not only braver and more enduring, but they were more selfless. I marvel that a soldier can fall on a hissing grenade to save his comrades, but I believe that every man who has known the driving impetus of combat has some small intimation of this greater love.

It is common in war for visitors from the rear to report with wonder on the increasing cheerfulness they encounter on approaching the front. I believe that they are reporting this phenomenon of intensified life and are experiencing it themselves. It is not, however, a constant emotion. For some, it never develops at all. In even the most steadfast soldier, it will at some point sink low, or fade altogether, leaving him aware only of his fears and of the nightmarish forms of death and destruction all around him. This is the breaking point, and it exists somewhere for every man.

Assuredly, that night I did not speculate on whether the shade of Old Jack might be drawn from the shadows to this battle-swept place on the coast of France, where the current bearers of the name of his famous command were in deep travail. History indicates that he would not have countenanced stopping but would have given his usual abrupt order: "Close up, press on." I cannot imagine disputing that awesome individual in person. But from this safe distance, I can quote another less-known pronouncement he made at the end of a hard and confused day at White Oak Swamp in the Seven Days battle before Richmond, when he told his commanders, "Now, gentlemen, let us at once to bed and see if tomorrow we cannot do something."

I believe that the day on Omaha Beach was as hard and confused as the one at White Oak Swamp, and rest from it was equally justified. In the early morning hours, I retired to a corner of the barn, wrapped myself in a stray rain slicker, and slipped into light and troubled sleep. The last sounds I recall were occasional shell fire, distant bursts of machine gun fire, and the low voices of an officer and sergeant of the 115th who had come to our barn about plans for a patrol.

The time was about two hours before dawn of the second day.

3

Saint-Lô

> To Choltitz, who commanded the LXXXIV [German army] Corps, it seemed
> that the battle of the hedgerows was a "monstrous bloodbath," the like of
> which he had not seen in eleven years of war.
>
> *Breakout and Pursuit*, Martin Blumenson
> Office, Chief of Military History

The 29th Division's immersion in this "monstrous bloodbath" culminated
at Saint-Lô. Here, too, emerged the nation's symbol of the price it was
paying in Normandy: "The Major of Saint-Lô," Tom Howie, killed on its
outskirts in the white mists of a sultry July morning and carried into the
ruins to lie in state with the flag as his shroud. All this, however, was six
weeks after D-day in the order of telling, and perspective requires interim
narrative.

The second day of the crusade in Europe, 7 June, came on windblown,
dripping. The battle that had growled and muttered at intervals through
the night stirred louder at first light. After washing and shaving at a horse
trough, we began what was to be a long and tasteless association with
K-rations — the precooked and canned combinations of largely unidenti-
fiable ingredients packaged in a waxed paper carton that, theoretically,
could be burned to warm them. Also in theory, eating the complete ration
provided a balanced diet. In practice, the soldier ate the part least offensive
to his taste and discarded the rest. For me, the sugar cubes were the most
familiar tasting, and, in the belief that they yielded energy, I consumed
them heavily, being driven only by stark hunger to the egg, meat, or dried

fruit mixtures. Next up the line of nourishment came the C-ration, which, in larger cans, required more extensive fire to heat and, in the front line, had usually to be eaten cold. My predominant memory of these foods is their pervasively metallic taste. More kindly remembered are the can openers: An entire army feeding from individual cans made these pieces of hinged metal essential instruments of war that were uncommonly efficient. Some wore them like religious medals around the neck; I daresay that many a soldier has kept his can opener, along with his dog tags, as a most personal memento of the war.

By 0500 on that second day, we had each made the best peace we could with K-rations and with the discipline of hygiene and, despite individual reluctances, were prepared to resume the war. A battalion of the 115th Regiment took over the attack at Saint-Laurent, and Major Bingham led the fragments of E, F, and Headquarters companies, one hundred or so strong, back to Les Moulins, where a few defenders were still holding out. The invasion had flowed inland around these few, until they were hardly eddies in its current, and they were ready to surrender; most we found to be Russians or Poles in German uniform, a nondescript lot for all the carnage they had caused.

I took a last look at Dog Red from the cliff top and recall that it resembled a huge, badly organized junkyard. An occasional artillery shell still erupted along it but scarcely interrupted the antlike activity among the piles of debris and the supplies still coming ashore. I turned away without regret as the battalion was ordered to Louvières, our D-day objective, on a schedule that had already slipped so far as to be forgotten.

We started inland in a short column of files on either side of a road that curved across a flat plateau of pasture and cultivated fields. The march was slow, as scouts at the head felt their way toward an inevitable meeting. A half-mile inland, we were alone on the road, and here the beachhead seemed vacant; the toehold of the crusade in Europe still extended barely beyond the waterline.

Our route passed occasional gray stone or stucco houses, all deserted, and vast bomb craters that should have been on the beach but were, instead, in vacant fields where they had disturbed, at most, the topsoil. Further along was a large complex of ancient brick farm buildings, walled together like a fortress. A young Frenchman in faded blue work clothes, beret, and sabots came out through a gate in the wall, and we exchanged mutually baffling Tennessee high school French and Norman country dialect about what he knew of the German forces in the area. Largely through pantomime and pointing at maps, we established that he had seen German positions dug in at Louvières. Late that afternoon, these were found to be occupied, but at about the same time an order came to countermarch to Vierville, where heavy German shelling was judged to be the precursor of a counterattack to regain the beach exit road. So back we slogged and took up a position among the jumble of stray units around Vierville.

I was sent on some forgotten mission that took me through the junction of the beach exit and coastal roads where the shelling had been concentrated. There is a dreadful sameness to such scenes: fragments of torn metal, masonry, vegetation, and bodies. The smell is of burned explosive, oil, cloth, wood, metal, flesh — a combination of odors that never clears the memory. All of these elements crowded the scene at Vierville, for the shells had hit into a jam of vehicles tailgating up from the beach, tearing and throwing them about. The wounded had been removed, but the dead were still there.

The scene held the unretouched countenance of war. As I picked my way through it, a clanking halftrack overtook me, and Colonel Canham, aboard with some of his staff, offered a lift. His bandaged hand, wounded the previous day, was in a dirty sling. With the slight upward twitch of his moustache that represented his smile, he asked how my company was for haircuts — the matter that had drawn the painful racking months before. I do not recall my reply but trust that I did not mention close shaves.

That night, I got around for the first time to the adjutant's job of posting the battalion journal. I have cited this as a memoir source and have said that, while helpful as to dates and places, it rarely touches its potential as a firsthand, front-line record. The entries for D-day, made that night by the pinpoint of shielded flashlight, set the sadly lacking tone and content: "Beach apparently not bombed by Air Corps. Three-story house at Les Moulins still standing. Enemy well dug in. Beach well defended." If history's Muse, Clio, happened to look over my shoulder that fateful night, she must have sighed in dismay, but perhaps not; she must now be reconciled to inept recording of mighty events.

There was no counterattack; the next morning, the crippled 116th, with some equally crippled 2d and 5th Rangers, struck westward along the coastal road to relieve other 5th Rangers who had been holding on at Pointe du Hoe for the past forty-eight hours

Major Fred McManaway, battalion executive officer, had brought in more 2d Battalion people whom he had located around the Vierville area (some had been caught in the shelling), and what was left of the battalion was now back together. About half of the riflemen, NCOs, and officers were dead or hurt; with some exceptions, few of those remaining had developed a passion for combat; most, I believe, found the battle already overly long. We did, however, continue as a diminished but still destructive force with lieutenants commanding the companies, sergeants and corporals in charge of platoons, and privates first class leading squads that were three- and four-men strong.

Even though now flash-aged veterans, we were not yet as combat-worthy as we would be. For example, a practice started of passing verbal messages from file to file down the column, and, as in the old parlor game, they arrived fully garbled: "Drop off a squad at the crossroad" became "Drag a signal across country." A heated protest passed back up the column, and this practice ceased; profanity transmitted with remarkable clarity.

The 3d Battalion, healthiest in the regiment, led the advance that uncovered Pointe du Hoe and the Rangers who had landed there at dawn on D-day, scaled the vertical cliff and then had hung on under hard pounding. Continuing that afternoon, we came up against a strong position dug in outside the fishing port of Grandcamp. An attack here was stalled until Sergeant Frank Peregory of K Company got in and cracked it single-handedly. He survived Grandcamp but was killed before his Medal of Honor was awarded.

In the battered town, I came upon Tom Howie, imperturbable as ever, seated on a low rock wall and marking a situation map with the regiment's present position, far short of the line we had intended to reach by then. Tom took the time to tell me what was known of the situation in the beachhead: All three of the 29th's regiments were ashore, but nowhere more than two miles deep into Normandy. The rumor that all the 111th Field Artillery Battalion's howitzers had been lost in landing was true, and, until it could be reconstituted, any artillery support that we got would have to come on reluctant loan. He said all this matter-of-factly. I nodded assent just as casually, so routine had bad news become. There had been nothing during the past days to rouse even momentary enthusiasm; I believe that spirits generally had settled at the level of dogged endurance, probably more practical under the circumstance than elation, which is always fragile and short-lived.

Grandcamp was secured, though stray rounds of small arms fire still zinged occasionally off its stone walls. It was here that the surviving part of the battalion's supply train caught up, led by Jim Bagley, whose lanky frame was so folded that only his ruddy face showed about the jeep's hood. He gave me a can of C-ration stew, which I stowed away against an opportunity to heat it.

That afternoon, I had occasion to go back along the route of our advance and on the way passed a gaggle of stragglers from a variety of units who had, with a common interest in avoiding the fight, come together around a farmyard water pump. The mucky ground was littered with the insignia of sergeants, corporals, technicians, and even the one stripe of privates first class. Inquiring of a furtive type the reason for this, I was told that the Germans were making targets of marks of rank. Without attempting to police the rabble, I went on my way. A mark of the battle leader — a Nathan B. Forrest or a Jackson (either Old Hickory or Stonewall) — is moral force to hold the faint-hearted to the fight. We who burn with a lesser flame may seek support in Shakespeare's vaulting lines for Henry V at Agincourt, beginning: "He who hath no stomach to this fight, let him depart . . . ," and going on to the classic, "we happy few, we band of brothers."

Henry V's personnel policy, provided him by the Bard, may suffice for small, elite units, and for great drama, but mass armies that have to stay with and win modern wars must make do with many who must be coerced to courage. I was not good at it, preferring the company of those who had stomach — however queasy — for the fight. Looking back down the years to those faithful few digging in around Vierville that dismal June afternoon, and then at those milling around in the farmyard, a short distance away, ripping off their insignia, I must conclude that never in war have the foolish, ugly antics of self-interest been more cheek-by-jowl with the supreme dignity of courage and selflessness than on the Normandy beachhead.

The night and next morning were spent around Grandcamp, and that afternoon we marched inland again, stopping near La Cambe on the Aure River. Before us stretched a wide expanse of water, the Germans having flooded the river valley by blocking its drainage canals. The 116th was now in division reserve, and we spent the next day in place trying to regroup battered squads, platoons, and companies into better tactical order. This effort ran into immediate opposition as squads, reduced to three and four men, still insisted on keeping their identity and opposed consolidation with others; men also declined promotions that meant going to another platoon or company. The past four days had developed powerful bonds between those who had supported each other through them. I believe that things were finally left very much as they were; soldiers who have carried the weight of the battle acquire considerable influence in such matters.

A second night was spent on the Aure, and I was awakened in its late hours by a light drizzle of rain and by a scream of "gas" from a nearby hedgerow. My first reaction was akin to the panic in the cry, for my gas mask had been ruined and abandoned on the beach. Then, more fully conscious, I recognized it as an alarm sounding from some soldier's nightmare, and my attention shifted to the rainwater collecting in the foxhole, causing me to clamber out and shiver through to daylight. We were living and moving in the stuff of nightmares, and cries in sleep reflecting this were not infrequent. I do not recall any action set off by these unconscious alarms, other than profane demands from neighbors that the hard-pressed dreamer keep his troubled spirit to himself. Word circulated some time later of a false alarm of gas attack sounded through the back areas of the beachhead, creating panic that added some humor, but no honor, to the annals of the crusade in Europe.

The next day, 11 June, the flood waters had receded enough to uncover a road crossing the valley, and we slogged across unopposed. The 115th was already over, and there were rumors, vague as usual, that one of its battalions had suffered heavily in a surprise night encounter with a German column. Unlike so many such rumors, this one proved to be true; the 29th was temporarily without one of its nine battered rifle battalions.

Marching out of the inundated area, we passed the scene of a small, vicious fight that stays in my mind because of a very young Ranger lying there wounded, waiting for a stretcher. He looked not more than fifteen or sixteen years old, but I remember more vividly the rage still smoldering in a pair of startling blue eyes. His dirty face, with a fuzz of beard, was streaked by what must have been sweat, for I do not believe those eyes ever shed tears. He was attended with considerable deference by two fellow Rangers who pointed to the top of the rise and told me the fight had been for a position dug in there. The wounded lad had assaulted it head on, and the wonder was that he was alive. Looking over the blasted and blackened position, I found a concrete mortar emplacement with a panorama of the terrain painted in color around its rim, including ranges and aiming points for various targets. Prominent among these targets was the road over which we had just marched, which was reason enough to admire the fierce young soldier.

After a muddy crossing of the Aure River, the 116th remained in division reserve until about noon of 12 June (D-day plus six). These few relatively quiet hours allow time for a more detailed look at the Norman *bocage* — the hedgerow country: its influence on combat and as the background to the Saint-Lô battle. I have said — echoing many another — that the hedgerows, rising above ground, dominated the war in Normandy in the summer of 1944, much as the trench systems dug below ground dominated the war on the western front, 1914–1918. My experience does not span the two world wars, as did that of General Choltitz, but I can concur in his judgment that the war in Normandy was a "monstrous bloodbath." To this, the hedgerow was a major, though passive, contributor. I am also certain that the combined skills of all the renowned military engineers of history could not have built a more effective system of field fortification than these thousands of interlocking earthen embankments that divide the fields and orchards of Normandy. And it was a system ready-made and waiting for a German army that fully understood its uses.

Varying from waist-high to over head-high, yards thick, topped with brush and trees, the hedgerows bound triangles, squares, rectangles, and odd geometric shapes left by generations of land division. The result is an intricate and baffling maze in which observation is limited and direction easily lost. For good military measure, this maze is threaded by sunken farm lanes, ideal for covered supply routes and for lines of defense. The sunken lane plays a heavy role in battle history: at Waterloo, Antietam, Fredericksburg, Shiloh. In Normandy, such lanes are not single, but legion.

Fortifications, of course, are only as effective as the will and strength of their defenders make them. The German army in Normandy was still formidable in both. Its lack of manpower was compensated by this terrain in which a squad could kill a company attack and fall back to position after position, each as strong as the one given up. The metal we were able to throw took its toll but attacking across field after field remained deadly beyond comprehension. It was a rare rifleman who survived six weeks of it unmarked.

The hedgerow maze is also a ready-made tank trap, miles in depth. Tanks on their own could get through it only at farm-gate openings, and these were covered by antitank guns, or by the very effective German bazooka. Under the pressures of necessity, the device of welding steel prongs onto the bow was developed, enabling a tank to plow off enough of the top of a hedgerow to lumber over. Like most improvising, this had its limitations. It allowed use of tanks in small formations, but no mighty armored sweeps.

We became enmeshed in the hedgerows directly after breaking through the beach defenses, and the surprise increased losses. New assault tactics had to be developed and practiced under fire, for in the year of intensive preinvasion training no mention was made of hedgerow warfare, as distinctive in its way as mountain warfare. This oversight tempers my admiration for those massive preparations. We were rehearsed endlessly for attacking beach defenses, but not one day was given to the terrain behind the beaches, which was no less difficult and deadly. This is hard to understand, for the planners had current aerial photographs showing the maze and its problems, and the written record of fighting there goes back at least as far as Julius Caesar.

That he sensed the invasion plan might harbor some such blatant oversight was, I think, indicated by Winston Churchill, who grumbled — worriedly, sarcastically, ironically? — that from the number of vehicles to be jammed ashore we were certain, at least, of outnumbering the Germans in drivers (he called them chauffeurs). Not too much should be made of this, I suppose, for it is hardly a unique failure. The obvious never bellows more loudly for attention than it does in war and is never more often ignored. The oversight in Normandy had to be redeemed by infantrymen in hundreds of small, unsung fields.

Twenty miles of this maze lie between Omaha Beach and Saint-Lô. The town is the capital and market center of the department of Manche; more important militarily, it is where seven roads congregate, and where there is something of an exit into the more open valley of the Vire River. The invasion plan called for the 29th to possess the town by 15 June — D-day plus nine — a timetable that events showed to be an extension of optimism into fantasy.

Its original plan badly dislocated (the terrain was a prime dislocater), the U.S. First Army designed a new one to rupture the German line and through it break out of the beachhead. The new plan was called Cobra, and Saint-Lô met its first requirements for terrain and road net on which armored divisions could coil and strike. The offensive, overall, involved twelve divisions in four corps attacking on a twenty-five–mile front. It was bitterly contested at every point, and losses were uniformly appalling, for the German command had an equal appreciation of road nets and of the advantages of keeping the Allied armies enmeshed in the hedgerows. The Germans had, also, a captured First Army field order designating Saint-Lô as a major objective, and this insured that the town would be defended with all the manpower and firepower that could be assembled on the hills and ridge lines that lay accommodatingly across its northern approaches.

Presuming to speak for those who fought there, and who knew nothing, at the time, of Cobra or of captured field orders, the battle was a boiling cauldron that no man entered without dread or emerged from unmarked. In the end, of course, the offense succeeded. Cobra struck, and a general advance was begun that, with some setbacks — notably the Battle of the Bulge — ended in less than a year with victory in Europe. The cost was high: Over forty thousand Americans were killed, wounded, or just disappeared unaccounted for. The Germans had losses perhaps half again as heavy. Saint-Lô, with all the farms, villages, and hamlets on the way to it,

77

was knocked apart. Over one thousand Normans were killed. Conservatively, then, well over a hundred thousand human beings died or suffered injury in the brief time and space that bounded the offensive. The Red Horseman and the Pale Horseman of the Apocalypse have reaped more bountiful harvests, but they could not have been displeased with this one.

Saint-Lô, as a battle, shared fully in the offensive's macabre marks of distinction. Its rank in history, however, is no higher than that heavily populated tier of major bloodlettings that have determined the course of campaigns, as opposed to the few Gettysburgs and Waterloos on which the fate of nations has turned. In keeping with this rank, it is destined for the footnotes of history, unlikely to be remembered beyond the life spans of the U.S. First Army and German Seventh Army veterans who fed its flames so prodigally, those who anxiously followed their fortunes, and the Normans whose lives and property lay in its path.

The 29th Division did battle directly for Saint-Lô as part of XIX Corps — a point incidental to this account, for a corps headquarters was to me a vague upper sphere with which I had no contact. Often, I was forgetful of which corps was currently directing our devoted efforts. I am sure that to a corps staff the 2d Battalion was little more than one of the many colored pins on its operations map, to be regarded with approval if it could be moved forward and with disapproval if it could not. In brief, XIX Corps and I were unmindful of each other as personalities.

My account of this great hurly-burly is that of a foot soldier who, while groping through it, knew little of what was going on outside the few hundred yards of front on which the 2d Battalion fought. I was vaguely aware of the other mighty blows being exchanged across Normandy, but, being fully occupied with my own microcosm of Armageddon, I paid them little heed.

Back now to 12 June and to the immediate hedgerow war that the 29th was waging along the Elle River, a shallow, narrow stream that marked the southwestern extent of the Omaha beachhead — at this point about ten miles deep into Normandy. Late that afternoon, the 116th was ordered back into the badly gaped battle line near the gray stone hamlet of Sainte-Marguerite-d'Elle. The rifle companies crawled up to the river line and came under heavy fire from the opposite side. The battalion command post was set up in a roadside ditch some hundred or so yards to the rear. Perhaps the term "setting up the command post" conveys something grander than it was in our post–D-day state: myself, a runner, the operations sergeant — who oriented the map board — and a signals sergeant who hung the field telephone by its carrying strap onto a protruding tree root.

Our ditch was deep enough to take some of the menace from the bullets that cracked occasionally overhead, and I daresay my heroes and I would have been content to sit out that hot, humid afternoon of the war there — passing on to the regimental command post, over the telephone, a graphic description of the fight. This actually required little imagination given the noises and the black smoke pluming up from two of our tanks that had been knocked out before we arrived.

Conscience told me that I should go up and get the battalion commander's estimate, and while I was coping successfully with this urge, the divisional chief of staff, a colonel, appeared striding down the road from the front. It being obviously improper to remain in the ditch and exchange good afternoons, I clambered onto the roadway and reported our identity. My lads, with a fine grasp of protocol in such situations, simply stood up in the ditch and looked vague.

The colonel, a big, square man, acknowledged my report and, looking us over thoughtfully, began a fatherly talk on the experience of combat. I recall him saying that entering a fire fight eased nervousness — something like the first action of a ball game. We listened respectfully, but we had been under fire for the past six days, and I doubt that he convinced anyone that this was a sporting event or obscured its terminal probabilities. His calm and his obvious good intent were more impressive than his logic, and he really caught our ears when he said that our objective was Saint-Lô, and that after it was taken the division would be pulled out for a real rest and refit. The part about a real rest got our instant attention — more so than what the taking of Saint-Lô might do for the crusade in Europe.

The colonel wished us luck, which we returned, and he continued down the white, dusty road. Inspired by his presence, if not by his exposition on combat, we gathered the map board and field telephone to move closer to the battle. En route, we passed the latest commander of a rifle company — its third since D-day — going in the opposite direction, toward the aid station, blood dribbling slowly onto the road from the fingers of one hand, hanging loosely by his side. We had served together for two years, but he seemed so intent on some destination — staring with fixed gaze straight ahead — that I did not stop him to inquire about his injury. By this time, a wound with which one could with honor walk out of the war was a matter of congratulations rather than condolence.

The command post was set up closer to the rising clangor by hanging the field telephone on another protruding bush, and reorienting the map board. The results of the explosive, cracking noises began to mount: Lieutenant Bob Hargrove, a young lawyer from Louisiana, and one of the battalion's three winners of the DSC on the beach, went down with a badly shattered leg; at about the same time, Lieutenant Bob Garcia, from California, commander of E Company, was also hit and evacuated. Both had proved battle-worthy; both were my friends; the tear in the already weakened fabric of the battalion seemed widening beyond repair.

Hargrove's injury took him out of combat and into a long period of recovery. Garcia's was less disabling; he returned to E Company at the siege of Brest, was again wounded at Würselen the following October, and was again patched up and returned. No better leaders in combat came under my observation.

As the long evening of double daylight savings time waned, the Germans pulled out. The 2d Battalion splashed across the narrow, knee-deep stream, formed up, and headed across country for our objective, Sainte-Claire-sur-Elle, about one-half mile away. Unknown to us, a German column was pulling back on a parallel route toward the defenses around Saint-Lô and, just outside the village, sideswiped our right flank company. There was a brief exchange of fire and the two columns pulled apart, the effect on the war being a few more killed and wounded. The battalion journal records that the day's brief action cost five officers and thirty-six men, a portent of what was to come as we closed on Saint-Lô.

With daylight, the battalion perimeter was pushed out to the south of the empty village, whose citizens had learned that bombing and shelling were the going price of liberation. The command post was set up in a vacant house, and here we stayed for several days in contact with German outposts, both sides remaining relatively quiet and killing few of each other.

Our wounded included Major McManaway, and, as the senior surviving captain, I was anointed to his place as executive officer. It was an advancement about which I could have few illusions, for it had become apparent that the principal requirement was simply to stay alive and in a reasonable state of mental health. There was understandably little outside competition for rifle battalion jobs that carried such obvious hazards. The responsibilities were enormous and the rewards intangible, resting mainly, I believe, in a feeling of being at the heart of the war and in the admirable company of those actually fighting it. Otherwise, a rear-area headquarters at that time offered the same pay, better hours, and much better prospects for a long life.

Other events of the stay at Sainte-Claire were a visit by General Gerhardt and the arrival of the first replacements for our depleted ranks. The general arrived with his usual pronounced impact at our command post on a humid afternoon in mid-June. Those who had not gotten away in time stood in attentive attitudes around the stained walls of the musty provincial parlor while he and Major Bingham sat and conversed in front of the empty hearth. I do not recall exact words, but the general indicated approval of our efforts, which was gratifying if the cost of achieving them were not considered.

That night, Lieutenant Elmer L. Faircloth, the new adjutant, and I met the trucks bringing the first replacements — vague shapes, laden with packs and weapons, who were hurried away behind guides to their companies. We had been clamoring for men, so I was surprised at a sense of regret as I saw them stumble away toward the front. Their efforts to maintain places and reach a harm beyond their conception appeared innocent and somehow pathetic; I felt an ancient among children, knowing and dreading what they were to meet.

The way to war of the replacement foot soldier in 1944 was hard, crowded, and dull: via training camp, troop ship, overseas depot; then, probably leaving any friends he may have acquired along the way, by truck and foot to join strangers in facing death or great injury. On occasion, he never completed the journey. There is the sad, short saga of a column of replacements caught by an artillery barrage while toiling to the front at Saint-Lô, ending the war and life for some ten of them.

On occasion, new men were fed into units actively locked in battle. Sent in by night and placed in among dark forms who occupied gravelike holes scooped out behind hedgerows, they could hardly have known where they were. The resident shades, if they spoke at all, did not slight the dreadness of the situation or overestimate anyone's chances of surviving it. Sometimes, a new man did die before dawn, and none around knew him by sight or name; he was probably unaware that his brief war was fought under a banner distinguished by more than a three-digit number; he may not have even remembered the number, and, without the sustaining strength of unit pride or comradeship, he had started battle reduced to the final resource with which every man ends it: himself, alone.

The replacement system improved as the war wore on, but I think it remained essentially a wasteful and impersonal distribution of men, disregarding the fact that it was dealing with the human heart. Those who went to war through this system and endured were good soldiers indeed.

While on the emotional nature of battle, I should deal with fear. I have firsthand knowledge only of my own, the chief manifestation being the stomach drawing into a cold, protective knot at the sound of shells whooping and screaming in my direction, and a reluctance to leave depressions in the ground. I like to believe that I dissembled these tendencies very well; however, I knew fear intimately and believe this was a fairly general experience; when I speak of courage, it is not in the sense of absence of fear, but in the disregard of it.

There was, come to think of it, another visit while we were at Sainte-Claire: brief but offering a lesson to heed. I was, at the time, in front of the command post when a jeep roared by headed for the front, a staff officer beside the driver waving as they passed. I was annoyed at the dust and noise and amazed that anyone should close with disaster with such apparent abandon. The jeep disappeared down the road, its route traced by rising dust, which halted simultaneously with a burst of German machine pistol fire just beyond our last outpost. Later, I asked the Stonewallers along the road why they had not stopped the jeep. The arrival, they said, had been too unexpected. As an afterthought, one added that, too, he did not see why "they" should not scout roadblocks for a change — logic unassailable on other than abstract humanitarian grounds.

Early on 16 June, we were relieved at Sainte-Claire and struck southwest through close, wooded terrain for Saint-Lô, to be brought up short and bloodily that afternoon outside the stone-clad hamlet of Villiers-Fossard. The discovery that this was a key German position cost a staff officer and thirty-four men — the equivalent of one of our nine rifle platoons at full strength, or, more nearly, two platoons at actual battle strength.

The officer, battalion S-3 (operations), died literally over my head: He was in the garret of a cottage looking over the terrain, and I, on the ground floor, was trying to locate our position on a mud-smudged map. A blast of rifle fire smashed into the attic, and three riflemen dashed in announcing that they had shot a German directly above me. At the same moment, blood began to drip through the ceiling, and on the upper floor we found him, his life already leached away. The riflemen left with stark faces, and I went to advise Major Bingham that we had lost the second operations officer since D-day.

The fight flared and crashed at intervals all afternoon. As dark came on, I returned to the command post where a tank, sent to support our effort, clanked up, and its commander asked, in a weary Ivy League accent, in which direction he should traverse his gun. I advised him that it was more important to cut the engine before he ran over some of the headquarters men sleeping along the track. At that moment, nothing short of the Last Trumpet could have roused them. As the battle settled to its strange nighttime mutter, we slumbered around the steel war cart, only sentries and the telephone watch awake to fight the unrelenting onslaughts of sleep.

The next day, the battalion clawed again at Villiers-Fossard and lost another officer and thirty-five men, including two first sergeants. Clearly, the place was not to fall to a lone infantry battalion and a single tank. A combined infantry, armor, and air attack was later required to crack it.

Early on 18 June, Colonel Canham came up with orders that we were to march that same day to the left flank of the division's sector in a general realignment for the push on Saint-Lô. The new position designated was about a mile in front of the village of Couvains and astride a north-south gravel road that, at its firmly German-held end, intersected the main Bayeux–Saint-Lô artery, one of the principal stretches of macadam for which the battle was fought. The march began that evening, and it was the cold damp of early morning before the companies were deployed along the new line.

There was much starting and stopping. At one halt, I sat down on what I though was a boulder but found soft and yielding — the flank of a dead hog or calf. Weary beyond revulsion or curiosity, I walked on. Toward the end, I became so vocal about the uncertain operation that Major Bingham suggested I do my job and complain less, and we would all benefit. I was immediately ashamed, and am now, at adding to burdens heavier than my own.

Finally, the rifle companies got into position and the command post bedded down along the road. An hour or so later, we were up, shivering in a soggy dawn, to take stock of the prospects the place offered for further survival. The date was 19 June, and here we were to stay until 11 July, either on line or in reserve, while XIX Corps gathered for the final blow at Saint-Lô.

Any position that the German allows you to occupy without a fight is unlikely to be a bargain; this one was no exception. The lifting ground mist showed us deployed along an east-west elevation that was dominated by a parallel ridge line to the south about fifteen hundred yards distant. The higher ridge was called Martinville after the farm hamlet on its crest; its western end sloped off into the outskirts of Saint-Lô. The enemy held Martinville Ridge and a defensive line well forward of it, up against our own positions. In order to take Saint-Lô, about four miles to our southwest, Martinville Ridge had first to be secured.

During the three weeks we stayed there, I had time to note that the two ridges corresponded in relative elevation and separation to Gettysburg's Seminary and Cemetery ridges at the point of the grand assault in the center. This was not a comforting comparison for a Virginia regiment so I did not mention it. Too, at Gettysburg, the Stonewall Brigade was occupied bloodily enough around Culp's Hill on the Yankee right, and missed — gladly, I am sure — the tragic glory of the finale in the center.

Martinville Ridge also culminated in a hill on its German-held right, called 192 (its meter elevation). To strain the comparison still further, Saint-Lô had its Round Top: Hill 122 on the left flank of the German defenses. South of Martinville Ridge was another elevation along which ran the Bayeux–Saint-Lô road; south of that ran still another parallel ridge. Into all of these elevations is now incorporated American blood and bone.

Hill 192, looming to our left front, was in the area of V Corps and 2d Infantry Division. I visited its top after the battle and was amazed that, with field glasses, I could look directly into some of the fieldworks we had so laboriously dug and occupied. Why the Germans had not used this advantage to swat us like flies on a table is a mystery.

The first day was spent realigning the positions that had been taken in the darkness and weariness of the night before. The command post was dug into the side of a deep depression in a field alongside the road. The site offered access and defilade and, after being covered with a camouflage net, served the purpose very well, though the first hard rain revealed that it also served exceptionally well its original purpose as a sump to drain the field.

Across the road to our left were the mortar pits of the heavy weapons company, and the sharp whang of their firing was fairly constant until the late June storms damaged the artificial harbors on the invasion beaches and reduced the ammunition supply. The reserve rifle company was also deployed along the left to cover the open flank between us and the 2d Division. A hundred or so yards to the front, the war was fought moment by moment by the other two rifle companies. Their lines ran along a sunken farm lane until it wandered off toward Martinville Ridge, and then the positions took to the fields. The battalion's four remaining heavy machine guns were posted at critical points, and our antitank guns were sited on a slope to the right of the command post, covering the road. Our fieldworks consisted of pits dug into the side of the sunken lane or hedgerows and held rainwater with the usual efficacy of holes in the ground.

About halfway between our line and Martinville Ridge was the farm hamlet of Saint André de l'Épine, which was quickly knocked apart by shell fire and then gained an evil reputation as a costly and unattainable patrol objective.

The terrain setting was completed by hedgerow-enclosed orchards and pastures. The orchards bore small, tasteless apples for making cider and its dissolute cousin, the potent applejack, Calvados. Much of the battle was fought under the apple trees, and the only way to have increased its natural obscenity would be for it to have been blossom season (flowering dogwood and peach trees were an often-mentioned memory of those who fought under them at Shiloh in April 1862).

War had touched this fair and fruitful countryside before we moved in and had left two of its modern mementos in the form of a crashed British bomber and a wrecked German armored car. More traditional leavings were a number of the huge black and white Norman cattle lying in stiff-legged and bloated final repose in the fields, contributing the chemistry of their decay to the already fetid atmosphere. Immediately after digging itself underground, the battalion buried the dead cattle, and the men performed the amazing amount of personal hygiene that can be accomplished with a helmetful of water.

To indicate thus that the 29th Division maintained a tidy battlefield is something like boasting of operating a neat charnel house, or it may sound a "jolly, hockey sticks" note, both of which I detest in accounts of war. It is a fact, however, that — with little interest in keeping Normandy beautiful or in ecologically sound condition — our lines were well-policed. No matter how dreadful the day he faced, the Stonewaller shaved, if there was any way to do so; whatever the state of his uniform, it was worn correctly; and his weapon was clean. None of this was spontaneous. Men faced with surviving the moment have a natural inclination to disregard personal appearance and to discard anything that is burdensome, caring not where it falls. The divisional commander ordained against this inclination, and, as I have noted, he had a marked ability to enforce his views.

Even directly after the war, I had difficulty ordering the events of the three weeks preceding the 11 July attack. Individual scenes are vivid but tend to tumble together without sequence, as in a troubled dream. One consistent memory, however, is of a bone-sagging weariness, the result of long strain that had no end in sight. Whatever the cause, all seemed affected — I noted young men around me take on the look and movements of middle age. Few of us had grown up in opulent ease, and, over the past three years, we had lived and trained in cold or heat, dust or mud; we had marched literally hundreds of miles, run and crawled over all sorts of terrain. The physical demands of the static period at Saint-Lô were no heavier, yet a walk across a field left me panting as after a sprint and climbing over a hedgerow was a labored thing. This physical weariness was accompanied by a restlessness that made sleep fitful; the effect was that of a motor racing to move a sluggish machine, or of trying to run in a nightmare with much effort and little progress.

Also affected was my ability for outward emotional control. One afternoon, a military policeman returned two soldiers who had hidden out on the transport on D-day to avoid Omaha Beach. The loss of friends on that day had now come truly home, and the sight of these two, who had skulked while their betters were being killed, triggered a great anger. They were short, scruffy men, obviously not cast in anything of a heroic mold. (Abraham Lincoln said that soldiers who fled the battle were not necessarily all coward but might just be victims of cowardly legs. I suspect the reluctance of these two extended above the legs.) I became excessively the Stonewall Brigade major in describing to them their moral deficiencies and expressed regret that they had not been shot instead of returned to the battalion. They stood without a word through this, and I ended by asking if they had anything to say for themselves. Yes, said one, they would like to go to another outfit.

Spluttering, I waved them out of the command post. It would be gratifying to report that they went on to redemption through soldierly deeds. The truth is, I do not know their fate but suspect they found their way safely out of the battle, as everyone who wanted it badly enough seemed able to do.

The high points of hazard during this period were combat patrols, artillery fire that crashed into treetops and hedgerows, and mortar rounds that plumped down to shower steel fragments for yards around. The combat patrols, led by lieutenants until expended, and then by sergeants, reduced to near nothing the life expectancy of all who took part. The patrols did little more than demonstrate the "aggressive posture" desired by "them" and proved that the German outposts were still no more than a hedgerow or so beyond our lines, which we knew in any event.

The mortars distributed their summons throughout the battalion area and were particularly dreaded because the shells approached with a whisper, in contrast to the warning banshee screech of incoming artillery fire. I recall on one remarkably fine day coming upon a young headquarters runner, lifeless in the grass. He was slightly built and looked in death like a boy dressed in a soldier suit who, tired of playing at war, had fallen asleep in the meadow, face serene and fair hair stirring in the breeze. A few yards away was the telltale fin of a mortar round in a black rupture in the sod. The two-wheeled death cart came, pulled by its attendants who of a necessity appeared ghoulish, and took him away. Thus casually did death arrive and life depart.

The executive officer of a battalion is important primarily in being next in line for command, but in the meantime his duties are comparatively light. I took advantage of this during the static period at Saint-Lô to travel to the rear on missions whose principal purpose was to breathe the easier air out of artillery range. One trip was to a field hospital to have some of the metal fragments acquired on D-day removed from my face. I had recently upgraded the wound by maintaining that the metal deflected a compass held to the eye for sighting. In truth, I never had occasion to make such a sighting, and those to whom I demonstrated the deflection were unable to detect it, but it sufficed as a reason. The operation did not take long, and I gave the surgeon a German P-38 pistol, a gift I later regretted as these pistols became greatly coveted.

Returning, I stopped by to see Colonel Craighill, who was commanding the corps replacement depot. He told me that his only son, a paratrooper, had been killed on the D-day drop. He said staunchly that his son's unit had accomplished its mission, but his eyes were not staunch. The depot was filling with replacements being accumulated for the Saint-Lô attack. From a distance, they also looked doughty and well-turned-out. Up close, I noted that they were already acquiring the intent frown of the front line. The nameless regret I had felt on seeing the new men arrive at Sainte-Claire returned; these, also, seemed too young and innocent for what they were about to face.

Another remembered scene took place on a Sunday, perhaps Pentecost. I was en route by jeep to the regimental command post and, near the village of Couvains, encountered a procession of young girls in white communion dresses, followed by their families in Sunday black, headed for an ancient, gray stone Norman church. We stopped to avoid dusting the procession, and a detail of signal men stringing lines along the road ceased work to stare. Just then, a stretcher jeep from the front, with a bandaged, broken load, crept by. Here were all the elements of a contrived scene of a war movie, but this one was real and its screaming incongruity etched it in memory.

About this time I was promoted to major, in keeping with my new job. The staff draftsman, who did map overlays, painted a gold oak-leaf insignia on my helmet, which turned out to resemble more a pale yellow sunflower. Collar insignia had not yet caught up with the battle, but a proper oak leaf was presented by the few remaining of the men who had given me the set of captain's bars when we embarked for England over two years before. I asked no questions about the source of the scarce leaf but doubt that it was acquired through any accepted channels. I wore it throughout the war.

Romance, so essential to a movie or television war script, did not surface at Saint-Lô. No beautiful French girl (nor even a homely one) of the Resistance appeared to guide us by a secret route into the city. Our only connection with love was by letter, but this was avidly pursued. I thought we wrote more extensively than we received, but this impression may have been gained from the disagreeable duty of censoring letters for mention of where we were and what we were doing. Aside from having to read personal mail, this was a time-consuming and, I believe, largely wasted effort. The Germans, a few yards to our front, knew who we were and did not have to depend on the unlikely chance of i ntercepting a letter that might tell them.

The censorship of World War II must make its soldiers' letters home about the dullest on record. Some showed a knack for pornography, but the only letters I recall distinctly were those of a quiet, older soldier to his wife, about the home they planned to build after the war. Letter after letter went into every detail of location and layout. I gathered that most of his soldier's pay and her war factory wages were being saved toward this. He was killed, of course. There can be few legacies more painful than that of being left with half a dream.

From this, and others I came to know, I would judge that the rate of dreaming per capita at Saint-Lô was high. Undoubtedly, many dreams were of gossamer, but at the time they all seemed possible, for this war — like all the others — was the Last Judgment on an old and wrong world and the Genesis of a new and better one. In the event, the good and bad parts seem to have maintained about their usual ratio, and I fear that the mortality rate among the dreams that sustained so many at Saint-Lô has been fairly elevated.

Any humor that arose was largely unconscious and appears in retrospect, such as the memory of being in the E Company lines when a German shelling started, with its sequence of scream-roar-crash endlessly repeated. Four riflemen and I, who were standing behind a hedgerow, did not stop to analyze the Doppler effect of the first salvo but dove into the closest trench, which, unfortunately, had been scratched out for only two. Artillery fire reverses the normal human tendency to strive for the top of the heap; instead, the object is to get to the bottom, so there is always considerable turnover. The cold sweat generated by the situation, and the hot sweat from intense activity in humid weather, mingled in the heavy woolen uniforms that had been worn since D-day, about three weeks before. This, and the all-pervading stench of high explosive, made the atmosphere around us heavy and penetrating — so much so that, when the shelling let up, a muffled voice from the bottom of the pile plaintively demanded: "Don't any of you bastards ever wash your feet?"

As the days wore away, the plan for the assault was refined and resources for it gathered. The battalions were rotated between the front and a reserve area where, in company with engineers and tanks, the tactics developed for attacking hedgerows were practiced. At high noon on the Fourth of July, every weapon in the front line, and every artillery piece, fired a one-round salute. I do not know what the Germans made of this — in any event, they did not return the honors.

The attack was finally set for 11 July. The XIX Corps designated the 29th Division to make the main effort, and the 29th opted to lead with its left flank regiment, the Stonewall Brigade. The attack was to be in columns of battalions with the 2d leading. We were to strike south astride the Couvains road to the crest of Martinville Ridge, then wheel right, or west, down a farm road that ran along its crest and into Saint-Lô. Simultaneously, on our left, the 2d Infantry Division was to go for Hill 192, and upon its success depended much of what we would be able to do.

As when we had been designated for the Omaha Beach assault, the news of this Saint-Lô assignment had a stimulating effect; it represented a distinction among our peers — one to be deplored with pride. Preparations were stepped up; replacements brought the battalion to about three-quarters strength; rehearsal of hedgerow tactics — learned at such great cost — was intensified; artillery and mortar concentrations were plotted for every possible target. The memory that even greater preparations for D-day had not prevented near disaster was still fresh, but planning acquires its own momentum, and once again we became confident of walking over the enemy, this time into Saint-Lô.

Crowning this confidence was a massive air raid that thundered out of a clear sky late one afternoon, about a week before the attack, to dump streams of black specks on and around the town. The specks translated into a constant, rolling thunder. Everyone watched as the majestic trains of bombers, trailing their white contrails like scarves, crisscrossed the target. To the soldier fighting in the dust and mud, this seemed a safe and clean way to wage war until black smudges of antiaircraft fire blossomed among the formations, sullying the white-on-blue patterns of contrails and sky. First one, then another, and still others of the brave caravans merged with the black smudges and tumbled toward earth. Still, it was all so far removed from the war we knew that I had trouble realizing that men were being burned and broken in those far-off machines. The tympany of the bombs was more familiar, and the knowledge that the enemy was caught in it gave a macabre lift to the spirits.

Spirits also received a lift from an issue of clean uniforms. As I have said, the uniforms we had worn since D-day, impregnated against blister chemicals, had a sour smell to start, and the addition of weeks of dirt, rain, and sweat gave them an overwhelming presence. The change to fresh ones must have done as much toward improving the air quality index of Normandy as had burying the dead cattle.

Altogether, it was a recharged 2d Battalion that made final preparations to jump off at 0600 hours on 11 July. A forward command post was dug in right behind the line of departure, which was the present front line; 50-caliber machine guns and the short-barreled guns of the regiment's Cannon Company were added to the front line to blast the first German hedgerows with direct fire. Tanks, fitted with the metal tusks to rip passage through the hedgerows, were to support the attack; engineers were to blow hedgerows that could not be so surmounted. Five battalions of artillery were to lay down twenty minutes of preparatory fire before the jump-off and then precede the advance with a continuing barrage.

By dark on 10 July all plans were complete, all resources assembled; I was confident that a battle-proven battalion could not fail. German artillery had been more active than usual that day, but I gave it little thought. When I crawled into my slit trench under a hedgerow in the assembly area about midnight, my main concern was what the tanks might do to our new telephone lines laid along the ground, and I had the belated thought that they should have been strung overhead.

Sleep was brief, awaking abrupt; for a source of early-morning nausea available to the male, I give you an unexpected enemy barrage, which has no right to be, crashing and quaking earth and air. This was not the single rounds and short volleys that we had been receiving, but a full-dress cannonade. My first resentful thought was: "Where did they get all those guns?" The sound was that of ton after ton of brick being dropped from great heights, and I looked out expecting to see the assembly area erupting in fire and smoke. Instead, the tumult was all off to the right; the trees around us were carrying on their timeless dripping in the ground mist.

Regiment could tell us only that the 1st Battalion of the 115th, about one thousand yards to our right, was under attack. The crash of artillery swelled, died, and swelled again. The lulls were filled by the tearing bursts of machine guns; tracer bullets streaked in crazy patterns across the sky. This clangor continued at varying pitches for over three hours, but only an occasional shell hit our sector. Later, we learned that the attack, by paratroops and engineer troops, had a local objective and was made in ignorance of our own pending effort. The 115th had a very bad night before containing and driving it off. It was a sobering demonstration, too, of the artillery the Germans could concentrate. Our loss was limited to the few hours' rest we might have had before what was certain to be a long stretch, and, indirectly, a rifle company commander who came streaking into the command post about daylight, carrying a wounded soldier on his back. This strongly built young lieutenant had been propelled by attrition to command and, so far as I knew, had done very well. Now, he insisted that he must carry the wounded man to the rear, and from his eyes it was clear that he would not command that day. He left with the man on his back, and we did not see him again.

Word came down that the attack would go on as planned. Bending as under tremendous burdens, the files moved forward through the ground mist toward the hedgerows from which they would jump off. The command post followed to the forward bunker. All was quiet until a rapid volley of thuds behind us announced the departure of the preparatory barrage. The shells sighed overhead to end their brief careers in din, smoke, and flying fragments on the German positions. From then on, salvo after salvo crashed along the front. Under cover of this noise, the tanks moved up and, sure enough, tore up the telephone lines as they went. The ear-shattering blast of high-velocity tank guns and the beat of machine guns joined in, until it seemed that sound alone would destroy everything.

Not so. At 0600 the artillery fire lifted to the German support positions, and the rifle companies, starting forward, were met by blasts from machine guns that had somehow survived the bombardment. The futility of charging machine guns had been proved often enough, so the slow process of beating these emplacements down was begun. The telephone line to regiment was relaid and along it came the incessant demands for reports. The lines up to the attack kept going out, and, to get away from questions to which I did not have answers, I went up to see the battalion commander, passing a swath of dead Stonewallers who had been caught by the spray of fire as they topped the first hedgerow.

The attack had progressed only two or three fields. Marking the limit of advance was a tank, and while I watched, a soldier climbed up behind the turret, apparently trying to see what lay ahead. As he raised up, a burst of bullets swept the turret, knocking him backward as though jerked with a rope. A pall of smoke hung over the fields, holding in the sweet, sickening stench of high explosive that we had come to associate with death. The green covering of Normandy was gouged by shells and tank tracks; blasted limbs hung from the trees; the attacking riflemen, visibly shrunken in numbers, crouched behind their farthermost hedgerow while volumes of artillery, mortar, and tank gun fire flailed the fields beyond.

Major Bingham told me to keep up pressure on the heavy 4.2-inch mortars to maintain fire on the ridge and to tell regiment that the advance would continue when it damn well could. I returned to the command post heavy with the thought that this was Omaha Beach all over again in a different setting. The shells rushing overhead to the ridge had lost their promise. German counterfire was hitting with considerable force onto some empty fields to my right, and I judged that our own efforts must be just about as effective.

But I had misread the battle. Soon, word came that the battalion had broken into a sunken lane that was the anchor of the German position. Part of the cost also appeared at the command post: two wounded company commanders on the way to the aid station. Of the four company commanders at the dawn's early light, there now, at midmorning, remained only one. Perhaps half the platoon leaders and sergeants were casualties. The losses in riflemen were heavy but uncounted; the battalion commander was now leading all that remained.

Whatever we had suffered, the Germans had fared worse. Once past the sunken lane, their defenses crumbled and the attack moved rapidly up the ridge. The command post gathered map boards and radios and, trailing assault telephone wire like an umbilical cord, moved after it, passing through the area of the battalion's suffering and into that of the Germans'. Our dead lay where they had fallen; the wounded had either walked or been carried out.

Advancing into enemy territory long denied you is like setting foot on an unexplored shore: You look around, wondering at the evidence of a strange and hostile people. In the lane and beyond, all was devastation, blasted and burned. German paratroopers, whole and in parts, lay about. It was difficult to reconcile these diminished, inert figures in round helmets and blood-soaked camouflage smocks with those who had been, that same morning, among the most dangerous fighting men of the war.

A long-barreled assault gun on its low-slung armored chassis, which had taken a heavy toll along our front, was now blackened and smoking. The stench of high explosive was heavy and nauseating. The battalion commander's orderly was nearby. As we paused in the lane, with its shambles of flesh and shattered equipment, he said with puzzled sadness, more to himself than to anyone around, "I don't understand it. I just don't understand what it is all about." He was enterprising at his job, helpful, not servile, and impressed me as a man capable of running a first-class Italian restaurant. His words must have echoed those on many a battlefield and in many a language; there could be no elation in a sight at once so brutal and pitiful.

We went on in the wake of the destructive force that had swept up the ridge, stopping by the ruins of Saint André de l'Épine to tap in a field phone to report our location; then, up the long slope and to the road that ran down its spine westward to Martinville and on into Saint-Lô. The rifle companies had made their sharp right turn astride this road, and in doing so exposed their left flank to the two German-held parallel ridges to the south. Evidence of what this was going to mean was near the turn in the form of stinking shell craters and more dead. The 2d Division's progress in taking Hill 192 had kept fire off our backs.

After clearing the turn, we halted to let the signal crews, toiling under heavy reels of telephone wire, catch up. While so disposed, a tall young lieutenant in a clean uniform and wearing the then much sought-after combat boots (we still wore leggings) strode by, upright and with purpose and not at our bent-back, trudging gait; obviously here was a general's aide from some remote "they" area. He wasted not a word, and hardly a glance, on our bedraggled crew, and someone behind me muttered that there went another bastard to collect his medal. This may not have been his purpose, but it was not uncommon for such people to come up for a quick visit and then claim a medal for "voluntary exposure to enemy fire."

Medals for valor can be acquired in ways that are passing strange and have but a tenuous connection with their intended purpose. The nation recognized the majority of those killed or wounded that day with Purple Hearts, and with the Combat Infantryman Badge for performing "satisfactorily" in ground combat; in a postwar spasm of conscience, the Bronze Star went, upon application, to holders of the combat badge. Measured against this, I take a jaundiced view of claims of valor for fleeting visits to the front on the basis of a job that did not require such exposure. The attitude that in war some should be constantly subject to death and dismemberment while others should not be — and should be rewarded if they are so momentarily — is as hypocritical a form of segregation as exists.

I did not see the lieutenant again; perhaps he walked on into the German lines and paid a due price for a useless gesture. The command post continued on down the ridge to where the rifle companies had come up against exhaustion and a German stand, still about two miles short of Saint-Lô. As the evening waned, the command post was dug in alongside a high rock wall next to the road, and here we remained for nine days as the battle reached the peak of dull, red fury that civilized man, alone, seems able to mount and sustain.

During the night, the Germans formed a new line that ran across Martinville Ridge, the two parallel ridges to the south, and the deep draws between them. The next day, 12 July, the 1st Battalion, committed in the deep draw to our left, made but little progress, as did the 3d, attacking south against the Bayeux road ridge. On the third day, the 175th Regiment attacked through our 1st and 3d battalions and made small gains at high cost.

The 2d Battalion went nowhere at all on this third day, and it was evident that its bolt had been shot; it could only stand and bleed. Familiar enough by then with the results of men's discharging high-explosive projectiles at each other at close range, I was still aghast at the rate at which the corpse carts and stretcher jeeps were trundling away the Stonewall Brigade. By the end of the first day, we were well below half-strength; by the end of the third, less than one-third remained on the ridge. As always, over 90 percent of the casualties were riflemen. Instead of three rifle companies, we mustered barely the equivalent of one; heavy machine gunners suffered to a like degree.

Again, the German losses were heavier. Their 3d Parachute Division, which took the brunt of the attack and fought so nearly to the death, lost 4,064 in three days; their 352d Infantry Division, perhaps not so do-or-die, recorded 984 casualties in two days.

On the evening of this fourth day, 14 July, the 2d Battalion was relieved on the ridge and went back for rest and partial refit near St. André de l'Épine. The kitchens sent up hot rations, and replacements arrived, bringing us back to just over half-strength again. Some of the replacements, however, were patched-up wounded from D-day, and, while possibly restored physically, the were not up to rejoining the battle.

General Gerhardt visited the bivouac area that evening and spoke to assembled representatives from each company, in his staccato fashion, about how well we had done. Faces lit up a bit, but I do not know if it was because of the praise or because the general added that after taking Saint-Lô the division would get a real rest. We had been depending on this for some time, but it was good to hear it from this man.

Somewhat revitalized, the battalion trudged back up to its old position on the ridge on 15 July. That afternoon, we and the 1st Battalion on our left were ordered to try, before dark, to break through to the hamlet of La Madeleine just outside Saint-Lô. The way was to be prepared by thirteen battalions of artillery and a fighter-bomber strike, nearly three times the firepower of the first day of the assault. As with any prolonged battle, Saint-Lô proved a magnet attracting more and more metal from both sides.

The weather was notably clear and bright, in contrast to the clouds and rain that had hung over the battlefield for days. The company commanders, all lieutenants, were assembled along a hedgerow, and Major Bingham told them what we were to do; unit boundaries were fixed and maps marked. Within the hour, the artillery preparation began and the fighter-bombers roared and dove in over the objective.

Whether it was this tremendous weight of metal crashing down upon a narrow front, or German command confusion, I do not know, but the attack broke through, and the companies took off in full career for La Madeleine with an élan to which even Old Stonewall would have had to raise his cap. A squad or so of the reserve rifle company, the command post, and heavy mortars were following when word came down to halt the attack and button up for the night. The effect was that of throwing a hard-running machine abruptly into reverse: The rear end skidded to a stop while the front end, consisting of the two attack companies, part of the reserve company, and the heavy machine guns of the weapons company, broke loose and kept going right down to the objective. Major Bingham took off at a run to catch them. Later, we learned that the halt order stemmed from "them," not knowing, or not believing, the extent of the success.

Uncertainty took over while command and staff wheels ground out the decision not to withdraw the companies, but for the rest of the Stonewall Brigade to fight on down and join them. In the meantime, German command and staff wheels must also have been grinding, for the gap that the attack had opened was rapidly closed, and so the bulk of the battalion was cut off.

Over the next two days, the position at La Madeleine, won at modest cost, became progressively more ominous. The Stonewall Brigade was in a poor posture to strike effectively; instead of a clenched fist, it now had a weak finger of two companies stuck over a mile deep into hostile territory. Halfway back, well out of supporting range, was the 1st Battalion, which had been halted intact; back on the original position were the 3d Battalion, which had been badly mauled in an attack that morning, and the remnant of the 2d.

Compounding the hazard of their position, the companies at La Madeleine had only the ammunition and rations that individuals had carried with them. Their only means of communication was by the artillery liaison officer's radio, and its batteries faded more with each transmission. Still impressed, however, by the day's success, I was confident that we would push through the next morning; I knew my outfit, and, with its commander there, I would bet on its being able to survive one night anywhere.

Events did not turn out exactly that way. The next day, 16 July, instead of attacking toward La Madeleine, the 1st Battalion had to fight for its life against German assaults. Its right flank company, along the ridge road, was blasted by a tank at point-blank range and was reduced within minutes to less than platoon size. The remnants of the 2d Battalion, still on the ridge, were caught in this hurricane of fire and noise that swept back and forth across the narrow front for hour after hour.

Late that afternoon, as the fury abated, I reached my personal depth of the war, and it has remained with me as only the events that mark the ultimate depth and height of one's life remain. I was alone outside the now-useless command post; the sun, setting behind Saint-Lô, glowed a dull, furious red through the smoke and dust raised by the shelling; tall trees along the hedgerows cast long, deep shadows; on the road was a smashed jeep with the flayed remains of the driver fallen half out of it; in the next field, a dump of mortar ammunition was smoldering, flaring brilliant white as the flames reached the powder increments. Here the shelling had stopped, but in the distance it still rumbled like far-off summer thunder.

The scene was *Götterdämmerung*. A Teutonic heart might have found it stirring grandeur. But not mine; not then. For suddenly I was overwhelmed by the conviction that my battalion was gone; irrevocably lost; destroyed. If the Germans could mount an attack that threatened to overrun this well-supplied position, what chance of survival had the understrength and undersupplied companies isolated in their midst? And if the battalion that had been the boundaries of my life for three years was gone, what chance had I? At that point, I was despairing of the war and uncaring of its purpose.

After dark, I was called to the regimental command post, with the staffs of the other battalions, to meet with the divisional commander. The dimly lit bunker was crowded and the air oppressive. The general, projecting his usual energy, reviewed the situation and said that while we had taken some hard knocks, the Germans had suffered more. He said that the 2d Battalion had survived the day without serious trouble, and that the attack to relieve it and take Saint-Lô would go on. He then delivered a harsh judgment on defeatism and self-pity, racking a hapless captain who had expressed discouragement. He did not know that at that moment, in the back of the bunker, stood perhaps the most despairing major on the Normandy front. Usually, this dynamic man's statement of purpose and direction lifted my spirits. But not that night; I could not believe that the 2d had survived such a day inside the German lines, or, perhaps to justify my own funk, I did not choose to believe it.

A new commander, Colonel Philip R. Dwyer, had just taken over the regiment from Colonel Canham, who had been promoted to brigadier and gone to another division. Our new commander assured the general that we were full of fight, or words to that effect, and the session was over.

I stumbled back through the dark to arrive at our position just as a heavy shelling set in to fill the night again with noise and concussion. My usually highly active sense of self-preservation must have been disrupted, for instead of diving into the nearest hole, I wandered aimlessly around the field, ears ringing from a nearby tree burst, the shower of fragments somehow missing me. My route passed the slit trench of Sergeant John Walker, who had been in the first platoon of which I had taken uncertain command. He called a warning and, when I continued on, jumped out and dumped me into the nearest hole and demanded that I stay there. So I did, and I recall little of the rest of the night.

The battalion surgeon appeared at daylight to inquire about the situation but showed more interest in what, he said, was my loss of hearing. He insisted that I go back to the division's medical clearing station for a check. What was left of the 2d Battalion had been attached to the 1st, leaving me particularly useless, and I made no objection. The surgeon at the clearing station, disregarding the hearing bit, had me swallow a blue capsule and then sent me to a nearby tent area. The capsule, reputedly capable of stupefying an elephant, was known popularly as the "blue-88," in tribute to the German's dreaded 88-mm gun. I barely made it to the tent and a blanket on the ground before falling off a high place into a deep, vacant sleep.

Eight or ten hours later, I climbed reluctantly back to awareness and found the tent had been removed while I slept. Along one side of the hedge-enclosed field stood a line of hapless-looking soldiers carrying mess gear, though there was no kitchen in sight.

While I was trying to sort all this out, a slightly built, sandy-haired lieutenant came up and pointed shakily to a bombed-out railway station barely visible in the distance. This place, he said, was too close to that target and ought to be moved. His voice trembled and he had a facial tic. Obviously, he was one with the line of dejected soldiers seeking comfort in the familiar ritual of standing in a mess line — even one that offered no food.

It came to me then, with a jolt, that this was the trampled field of the defeated in spirit; the division's way station for the emotional wreckage of the battle, the victims of what was called combat fatigue. Here was determined who was salvageable for further war, and who was to be discarded into the teeming rear areas. No *Götterdämmerung*, this; no twilight of the gods full of the grandeur and thunder of noble death. This was a place of whimper and cringe; the skid row of the battle zone. I had heard of it, and my offhand judgment had been that it was a mistake to cater to this extent to weakness. Finding myself there was a shock such as I had not experienced on Martinville Ridge. Now, I can see that field of the defeated as an essential part of the awful scene of Saint-Lô. These abject spirits were the counterpoint to those enduring on Martinville Ridge; their weakness accented strength as death accents life.

The answer to my own shame at having slept through my battalion's agony at such a place was to flag down a ride back to the ridge. Leaving that field physically was a matter of minutes, but emotionally it remains with me; I must always wonder how truly I belonged there.

Back on the ridge, the battle was in a perceptibly lower key. Where salvos of shells had been crashing in, there were now only random rounds. Avoiding the regimental command post, I returned to where I had left my people and found them still in place. Through consideration, or perhaps because too much else had occurred that day, no one mentioned my absence. I did not bring it up.

There was much news: That morning, 17 July, about the time I had left, a 3d Battalion attack had reached La Madeleine and found the 2d in relatively good shape, still unaccountably ignored by the surrounding Germans.

The other news was that Tom Howie, commanding the 3d, had been killed by a mortar shell fragment shortly after reaching La Madeleine. I have said that he combined to an uncommon degree the kindness and courage that would have better become us all. In mourning Tom Howie, I grieve for all for whom life and laughter ended at Saint-Lô; and, by some projection, for those for whom it has ended since.

General Gerhardt, who was imaginative as well as arbitrary, had, I suspect, come to realize the stature of the man he had once relieved of command. For whatever combination of motives (he was not a simple man) he had the flag-draped body taken into Saint-Lô when it fell, two days later, and placed high on a bier of rubble in front of the town's shattered Notre Dame. News stories and photographs followed, and Tom Howie, who had started the attack with a vow that he would reach the city, became "The Major of Saint-Lô" — the symbol of the battle. Many who mourned the fallen soldier at the time may now have forgotten, and new generations never have heard of him at all, but the story stirred the United States to no small degree that July 1944: A classic tribute to a worthy warrior, rising above the murk of a long, ugly war, caught the imagination and the heart. "The Major of Saint-Lô" inspired editorial tributes and one of the few poems of merit to come out of the war, factually in error, but true in its captured feeling. There are now memorials to Tom Howie in the rebuilt Saint-Lô, at the Citadel in Charleston where he was a star athlete, and another at Staunton Military Academy, Staunton, Virginia, where he had taught and coached football.

It is ironic that the qualities that made his death mourned and marked had served him so badly in the hard climate in which we trained before D-day, and then had taken him to his final appointment at La Madeleine. In daring, unsparing demand upon himself, and in thoughtfulness of others, he resembled Turner Ashby, commander of Stonewall's cavalry in the halcyon days of the Valley Campaign of 1862. Stonewall was harsh in his judgment of Ashby's failure to drive his troopers as hard as the infantry was driven and wanted to relieve him of command; but he wept, and the South wept, when Ashby was killed, as of course he was, the nature of such soldiers making death in battle fairly inevitable. Through knowing Tom Howie, I feel I know Ashby and the gallant-hearted and selfless of their kind in every army in every war. They do not finally win wars; those who are arbitrary and demanding, as well as brave, do that; but the Howies and Ashbys add a note of grace to a generally brutish scene, and for this they are loved and remembered.

My last memory of Tom is a brief contact on Martinville Ridge perhaps three days before he was killed. It is typical of his manner. The battle was at its height of violence and confusion. The 2d Battalion pioneers, for some forgotten and probably misbegotten reason, had planted antipersonnel mines along our front. Tom, now in command of the 3d, objected that these were more of a danger to our posture of attack than to the defending Germans. Criticism from another outfit, justified or not, was not graciously accepted in the atmosphere of the ridge. But no offense would be taken at a man who spoke as quietly and calmly under the shelling then going on as he had when I had first met him three years before, when nothing like this had existed in our most fevered imaginings. An agreement about removing the mines was reached, and he left with a smile and a wish of good luck. I never saw him again.

The Germans could, perhaps, not notice the fragmented 2d Battalion at La Madeleine, but the arrival of the 3d was enough to attract deadly attention. The mortar round that killed Tom Howie was followed by a day of heavy shelling and attack; the last one, late in the day, was broken up by a spectacular concentration of artillery, and by fighter-bomber strikes against the German tanks in their assembly area. Even so, the day's end found both battalions low on ammunition and with many dead and wounded.

But now the tragedy of Saint-Lô was moving to its close. For the final act, the devastated town was the stage, with XIX Corps divisions gathered above it on the inner slopes of the hills to the north and east. On the afternoon of 18 July, a 29th task force, built around the 1st Battalion, 115th Regiment, broke into the ruins and raised the division's flag. At about the same time, the Stonewall Brigade opened a supply corridor to La Madeleine, and evacuation of wounded and dead was begun. Tom Howie's body was carried into Saint-Lô. The town remained under heavy German artillery fire, and a rare bombing run by Luftwaffe planes added to the casualties of the task force holding it.

On 20 July, the 29th's sector was taken over by the 35th Division, which had been heavily engaged on our right. The 29th's units began moving back to the promised land of corps reserve near Sainte-Claire-sur-Elle. The division had been in combat continuously for forty-five days at a price of over seven thousand casualties; in effect, its nine rifle battalions had been used up about twice over.

There remains only a brief epilog.

The 2d Battalion departed the battle by foot on 19 July from La Madeleine to the ridge road. While waiting for it, I took a last look around the now quiet battlefield. Salvage crews were at work, and much of the wrecked equipment and weapons had been removed. But the deep wounds in the land were undressed and gave the appearance of verdant desolation. The base of every hedgerow was scalloped with holes, for no man had stopped even momentarily without digging in. Practically every hedgerow had been fought for, plowed by shells and gaped with raw passages for tanks. Whole trees were blasted down, shattered limbs hung from others. The sweet, sickening smell of high explosive persisted in the heavy air.

While I was looking and wondering at all this, the battalion in column of twos, Major Bingham leading, appeared toiling up the slope. The column was pitifully short; at first I thought it was only one company and that the other would follow. Then I realized that this was all there was, and the memory still dries the throat and stings the eyes.

I had seen the great, gray ships of the D-day armada — the largest ever assembled — stretching to the horizon in every direction; and I had often seen in England majestic fleets of Flying Fortress bombers returning from runs over Germany, tragic gaps in their formations, and, limping behind them, planes with one or two inert propellers. These were scenes awesome in power and portent. But, for a sight to grasp and hold the heart forever, I give you a decimated infantry battalion lurching out of battle, bowed with a mortal weariness and the weight of all it has endured. This is not a drama supported by mighty machines, but of ordinary men alone, who have achieved an extraordinary triumph over their fears and vulnerable flesh. For me, all other sights must pale beside it.

I joined Major Bingham and told him of arrangements for the bivouac. The brief column trudged on toward the Couvains road. Behind us, the mists of time and of on-rushing events began to gather over Saint-Lô.

4

Pursuit

> Between the physical fear of going forward, and the moral fear of turning back, there is a predicament of exceptional awkwardness, from which a hidden hole in the ground would be a wonderfully welcome outlet.
>
> *Battles and Leaders of the Civil War,*
> Union Army soldier, American Civil War

While the 29th rested in the promised land of corps reserve, the spearheads of Cobra gathered some ten miles to our south and west. We were unaware of this or that the First Army was disappointed that the July offensive had not gained better positions for Cobra's launching. Our response to this complaint, had we known of it, would have been that the complainers should have a go at a few hedgerows themselves — not a logical reaction, perhaps, but a natural one; the two are often at odds.

On 25 July, Cobra made do with the ground that had been provided west of Saint-Lô, along the Saint-Lô–Périers highway. Almost magically, it must have seemed to the Allied public, victory in Europe became sure and near, for within weeks their armies broke out of a shallow beachhead and rolled, seemingly unstoppable, across Normandy, Brittany, Flanders, on to Paris, and up to the borders of Germany itself. But here, braked by worn-out men and machines and an outrun fuel supply, the advance slowed and halted. In September, an effort was made to regain momentum by an airborne assault to turn the Rhine River barrier at Arnhem, the Netherlands, and open a way into the Ruhr. The courage of the airborne troopers was unable to redress the miscalculations built into this operation, and it failed.

The dark winter of the Ardennes followed, and it was returning spring before Germany was finally reduced to the smoking, starving ruin of defeat.

During the August progress of arms across France, however, any suggestion that the end to five years of devastating war could be so delayed was considered unpatriotic. Such a charge could not be laid to the Allied press and radio. The liberation of towns and destruction of large enemy formations (unfortunately, the two often overlapped) were trumpeted daily in stark black and white: valor and daring versus, at best, a diabolical cunning. A sense of swashbuckling abandon was conveyed, something of a game of Allied hounds coursing the German hare that scurried and darted about in a doomed effort to escape.

Perhaps a distant perspective of the giant scene gave this impression. Close up, however, at the armored and infantry points of the pursuit, the sensation was not that of chasing a hare but of following a wounded tiger into the bush; the tiger turning now and again to slash at its tormentors, each claw drawing blood.

The 29th joined this battle on 28 July, three days after the massive Allied air bombardment hit the German lines on a four-mile–wide front west of Saint-Lô, and Cobra struck, succeeding beyond all immediate expectations. It developed into the breakout from the beachhead, and then into the great pursuit that at its height involved four Allied field armies, French Forces of the Interior, and all the Allied air forces in the European Theater. Fighting rear-guard actions and attempting to escape this onslaught were three German field armies and what remained of the Luftwaffe. On 15 August, the Allied invasion of southern France added another front to the massive battlescape.

On a battlefield of such enormous proportions, the actions of a single battalion can provide only a vignette: a small, closely cropped scene from a giant canvas of fire-breathing columns, writhing and twisting across a fair French countryside, trailing broken men and machines, smoking villages, and trampled fields. This battalion scene, so relatively minute in time and space, covers fourteen days and some fifteen straight-line miles from the village of Moyon to the ancient town of Vire; in width, it rarely measures more than two hundred yards. It does not hold the extent of carnage and destruction of the Argentan–Falaise scene where the German Seventh Army was largely destroyed, or that of the German counterattack at Avranches, nor does it hold the tearful jubilation of the liberation of Paris. But it was not composed without pain, and I believe it to be a fair sample of much of the great pursuit. No swashbuckling column we, but a dogged, trudging one, at times creeping and crawling.

In addition to the always high list of emotional casualties, the Stonewall Brigade's fifteen miles cost over one thousand killed and wounded, of which the 2d Battalion bore its about one-third share. This was not excessive by the standards of Normandy, and it was light compared to the more than thirty-five hundred Stonewallers left along the twenty-mile stretch from Omaha Beach to Saint-Lô. But, to lose within two weeks more than one third of an actual strength of about seven hundred officers and men was enough to cause an immediate hurt militarily, and a lasting one personally.

The eight days between taking Saint-Lô and joining Cobra were spent by the 29th in refitting with men and matériel. The 2d Battalion bivouacked among gnarled apple trees in orchards outside the village of Sainte-Claire-sur-Elle, which we had taken in the attack just over a month before. The luxury of hot meals, showers, and clean uniforms, and of being away from the immediate vicinity of death and destruction, obscured the discouraging fact that the crusade in Europe had advanced little more than twenty miles during the past month of hard fighting and heavy losses. There were vague reports of the 20 July attempt to assassinate Hitler, and a momentary hope that this might mean the collapse of the German army, but nothing came of it and it was accepted that the war would have to be fought out the hard way.

The weather since D-day had alternated between damp cold and sultry heat but now turned pleasantly warm and bright. The sickening odor of cordite that had infected the countryside had blown away, and our orchard was green and summer-smelling. Through some logistical nonsense, athletic equipment was among the short supplies of ammunition and food still being brought in over the invasion beaches, but though a packet of it had arrived at our bivouac, it lay where it was dumped for there was no interest in playing games. Not so with the motion pictures that ran all day in a blacked-out barn, the film spotty and jerky from constant use. These wartime films, like wartime writing, projected a streak of blatant unreality, but they were avidly attended, for this was the tenor of the times and we were all attuned to it.

A Red Cross canteen truck also appeared at intervals with two American women attendants to dispense coffee, doughnuts, and paperback editions of books. The doughnuts had the weak wartime flavor of rationing, but some of the books were full-bodied. There is a pleasant memory of lying in the orchard grass on soft summer evenings reading MacKinley Kantor's *Long Remember*, a novel woven into the historical fabric of the Gettysburg battle. A chasm of time and circumstance separated Gettysburg, 1863, and Normandy, 1944, but I found it bridged by the casual and mindless unconcern with which the armies at the two places and times wreaked havoc on each other and on all about them. Armies of all time must be so linked, and by a common hodgepodge character of gallantry and rascality, courage and cowardice, compassion and cruelty.

Long Remember's noncombatant hero somehow managed to be present (pursuant to a love affair) at most of Gettysburg's critical moments; in fact, he toured the field before, during, and after the battle. This was hardly more implausible than much I had observed of war, but I did balk at his getting up Culp's Hill and into the Yankee lines on the second day, via Kantor's imagination and typewriter, after the Stonewall Brigade had tried it and failed in reality.

I have kept this copy of the novel, and its yellowed pages bring to mind the apple orchard outside Sainte-Claire-sur-Elle more vividly than they do Culp's Hill, Pickett's charge, and the high-water mark of the Confederacy.

Another book, *Forever Amber* by Kathleen Winsor, was the shocker of its day, and in such demand that I was able only to skim through it. I recall it as the tale of a village wench of Old England who employed her considerable charms most effectively on royalty.

The tension and fatigue of the forty-five days of battle just behind us gave way to lethargy, and given our general's attitude, this was a condition that would not continue. On the second day in reserve, he ordered a training schedule that included close-order drill. The battalion dutifully and profanely tramped, by platoons and companies, over rough pasture, soon wearing the sod through to dust. The shared sweat and temper that this raised helped meld the new men in with the veterans. Not long afterward,

First Lieutenant Cawthon, student at the Infantry School, Fort Benning, Georgia, December 1941.

2d Battalion staff during the siege of Brest, August 1944. Author in foreground, without helmet; Captain Si Johnson (S-3) second row, right.

Thomas D. Howie, as captain, destined to become the "Major of Saint-Lô" and receive the nation's tribute when he was killed in battle on 17 July 1944. Courtesy of Mrs. Sally Howie McDevitt.

Captain Tom Dallas (left) and author at Camp (now Fort) A. P. Hill, August 1941.

The forceful Major General Charles H. Gerhardt commanded the 29th Division throughout its campaigns in Europe. Courtesy of the National Archives, Washington, D.C.

Colonel Sidney V. Bingham, Jr., USA Ret. (center), with his driver, Pat Carusco (right), and "body guard," Bruno (left). Photo taken in Germany in early 1945. Courtesy of Colonel Bingham.

This shell-wrecked house marks the landing area of the 2d Battalion headquarters' boat teams on Omaha Beach. Courtesy of the National Archives, Washington, D.C.

Memorial to Major Thomas D. Howie, "The Major of Saint-Lô," erected in Saint-Lô, France, by its citizens. Courtesy of John R. Slaughter, sometime sergeant, the Stonewall Brigade.

Street of Dyers (rue aux Teintures), Vire, following a D-day bombing, and then the battle for the town on 6 August 1944.

the general also ordered that squad leaders recite the names and jobs of their men on demand, and he demanded this frequently, for there had been too many casualties unknown by name by their leaders.

Lethargy got its comeuppance on a dull July afternoon at a training session on hedgerow assault tactics. Little attention was paid to this requirement other than to assign a company to run a squad demonstration for the battalion. The company commander was new and relied on a sergeant who had been in the hedgerow fighting to stage it. The sergeant was a minor example of a type that the processes of combat throw up at every level: momentarily assertive and vocal, attracting brief attention, and then disappearing. On the whole, I noted, the quieter ones wore better, barring mortality, which dealt impartially with all types.

The sergeant's demonstration was not a model for the Infantry School. The battalion, trailing along like the gallery at a golf tournament, could see little and hear less. Awareness that more direction should have been given to the assignment peaked as the general arrived unexpectedly, with his usual velocity, took it all in with a glittering eye, and delivered several pungently phrased judgments in rapid order. The price for such a lapse during pre–D-day training could have been harsh and immediate, but, as a battalion that had pulled its combat weight, we got off with blisters. It was, however, enough to get us back on the job and to give the troops further cause to wish the war over.

Other scenes emerge from the shifting memories of that eight-day interlude. One is of sending a detachment of veterans to represent the battalion at the division's memorial service for its dead in the newly established La Cambe military cemetery. On their return, I thought I had never seen such somber young men. Each had one friend or more in the newly mounded graves; a corporal told me in a controlled voice that it looked as though a whole division were being buried there.

On another balmy evening, a section of the division's band gave a concert in our orchard. The bandsmen puffed solemnly on wind instruments or, equally solemnly, rattled traps and drums in their version of the Glenn Miller style. It was pleasant, but not enough to exorcise the presence of the war that lay so closely behind and so immediately ahead.

So far as we could foresee, the small, deadly battles for one hedgerow at a time, which had been going on since D-day, would continue indefinitely. Superiority in manpower, firepower, and air power assured the taking of that next hedgerow, provided the price was paid, but then there would be another, and another. This was the close-up, ground-level view of the war. At First Army headquarters, which dealt in larger views, plans were being completed for Cobra, whose first blow was to be a massive air strike to blast a corridor seven thousand yards wide and twenty-five hundred yards deep through the German defenses that fronted on the Saint-Lô–Périers highway. Four infantry and two armored divisions were then to attack to complete the breach.

It was just as well that we knew nothing of these plans, both for security reasons and because of a controversy between the ground and air staffs over the direction of the bombers' approach to the target area. The argument centered on safety for the attacking troops from bomber miscues, and argument such as this always disturbs the foot soldier, who figures it means he is going to catch it either way. First Army wanted the bombers to come in parallel to the front, using a long, straight stretch of the highway as a bomb safety line. The air staff wanted the approach to be from directly over our lines, perpendicular to the highway. As can happen when single-minded, forceful negotiators disagree, each side apparently thought it had won its point.

Cobra was to be launched on 24 July, but, after a portion of the bomber force was airborne from England, it was decided that dangerously poor visibility over the target required postponement. Some bomber formations did not get the recall signal and made their runs, coming in directly over our lines, a number of bombs falling short into the assembly areas of the infantry poised for attack, causing casualties and disruption. The next day, with better visibility and added precautions, the air strike went in again in full force, using the parallel approach. Again, however, human error showed its amazing versatility: Bombs were again dropped astray into the assembly areas and there were more casualties, including the general in command of ground-forces training — a power in the early wartime army.

Despite this, the infantry advanced and wedged a way into the bomb-wracked defenses. Cobra was under way and soon promised significant results. The sulphurous war of words that had broken out between the ground and air staffs over fault for the bombing errors was overlaid by the sweet smell of success.

I recite this much well-worn history to develop a facet of the infantryman's self-image: that all things somehow worked against him, even those designed to help. We had constant occasion to appreciate Allied air power but were also wary of it; some claimed it was safer to be on the bombing target than near it. A rare miscue by our artillery in dropping shells short was taken as proof by the foot soldier that not only the enemy was careless of his life.

Still ignorant of Cobra, we watched the planes go over and heard the distant, rolling kettledrums of their carpet bombing. Then came word of the offensive, and an alert order to join it on 28 July. Camp was struck early that morning, and then we waited until late afternoon for the trucks to convoy us to the front, exact location not known. I closed the rear of the motor march and so watched the trucks pass, still at careful sixty-yard intervals, loaded with serious-faced young men seated on fold-down benches on either side, rifles between their knees and packs stacked in the middle. Standing against the cab of each truck was an automatic rifle man on lookout for the Luftwaffe that had rarely appeared. Watching the trucks pass, I was again impressed by how little of the "old" — pre–D-day — battalion remained; those who were still there stood out by indefinable expression and posture.

The convoy trundled slowly down the dusty road, which was bounded on both sides by tangles of communication wire and broken hedgerows. Saint-Lô was a barren desert of broken masonry through which a roadway had been bulldozed. Here the convoy stalled in the enormous traffic that trails a major advance. The 2d Armored Division had been added to Cobra's fangs, and the pressure of its supply train compressed the sixty-yard intervals between our trucks until we were head to tail, lurching forward a few yards at a time toward a destination south of the city. Sitting in the middle of such a bountiful target was uncomfortable but proved uneventful; German artillery still within range was apparently more concerned with the forward edge of Cobra than with its rear.

After two hours, and about five miles, we were deposited by the roadside, and the trucks were turned about and roared away with what seemed undue relish. Again we waited, while a warm, still, and very dark night came on, the southeastern horizon glowing redly at intervals with gun flashes. It was near midnight before destination orders arrived by a jeep that crept toward us, cat's-eye blackout lights glowing evilly. The battalion formed up and started down the dusty road that in places stank of burned cordite. After two hours, the march became a plodding progress of men more asleep than awake. All traffic had disappeared; we were in a Stygian void, treading a shade-lighter line of roadway; even the war had stopped growling in the distance. About 0300, the assembly area was reached and the companies stumbled off into the fields.

Then it was discovered that Headquarters Company, bringing up the rear of the column, was missing. I told the commander that I would find it, and he observed that this was a damn good idea. I started back over our route, looking for what amounted to a moving black dot in a vast expanse of darkness. Sleep was becoming more and more the end of all desire, when I literally collided with Faircloth at the head of his trance-walking company. There was a mumbled exchange over not having heard the start signal at the end of the last ten-minute break and we trudged on to the assembly area. The commander was relieved that the lost had been found and said nothing further about how it had happened. On this happier note, I left the world and its foolish war for the incalculably greater attractions of oblivion.

Awakening came shortly after dawn with the blast of a rifle shot from an adjoining hedgerow, where, it developed, one of the new men had wounded himself in the foot. He moaned in shock and pain that it was an accident; whether so or not, he was our first, and inglorious, casualty of Cobra. The condition of his foot indicated poor-quality premeditation, if such it was.

Drifting away and out of the battalion portrait are the furtive shapes of stragglers, a few with self-inflicted wounds, many more who simply left. I have mentioned these but have not dwelled on them; but they are too many to ignore or to sketch in around the edges, blurred so as not to detract from an overall image of heroic endurance. I have said that fear in battle is pervasive; physical and emotional fatigue drags constantly at every fiber.

Tolerance to this fatigue varies, of course, between individuals. When a soldier's threshold is overreached, he becomes disabled. The factors determining this tolerance are many and interacting. Innate pride and loyalty are basic ones that can be reinforced by strong leadership and hard training. By the same token, poor leaders and training cancel out any amount of native courage. Also significant is the battlefield performance that the nation demands. In World War II, this was not exacting. We served under Articles of War that decreed punishment up to and including death for unworthy acts of omission or commission in the face of the enemy, but of the thousands who committed such acts, only one poor soul was singled out for execution. It was as if the nation found it had enough men willing to fight the war and so avoided the troubling responsibility of harsh measures against the reluctant. In some cases, executing a man for cowardice is like killing a cripple because he cannot run, but I believe many are as brave as they are required to be.

The German army required it and was not forgiving of those who failed. Even with disastrous manpower shortages, during the first half of 1944 some four thousand soldiers — the equivalent of a regiment — were executed for military offenses; this at a time when the Wehrmacht field army command was reduced to allocating platoon-size replacement units. During the last months of the war, as the German situation became ever more desperate, execution squads patrolled behind the lines and hanged, out of hand, soldiers caught away from their units without urgent battle reason. There is no record of their toll.

The German people — either through fear, disaster-induced numbness, or conviction — accepted this. The American people would not have been accepting; not in that war, nor in Korea, and certainly not in Vietnam. The one American soldier — an infantryman — executed by firing squad in World War II for desertion in the face of the enemy was unfortunate in having left his unit during the bitterness of the Ardennes winter battle, when it seemed for a time that, if more soldiers did not stay with it, the battle would be lost. His was a pathetic example, for, by the time he was required to serve it with his life, the battle was again enough in hand to be left to those willing to fight it.

By 1944, our infantry battalions were composed largely of draftees. But, given the lack of coercion applied to keep them there, they were draftees for the army and volunteers for the fight — many doomed by their own courage. World War II constituted a human winnowing process that discarded much that was usable for battle, I believe, had the process been made finer. Also significant is the battlefield performance

The 2d Battalion started southward that morning, feeling its way through a milky-white ground fog that lay over fields and orchards, damp and cool. The regiment's objective was a sector centering on Moyon, reported sparsely held by the 2d Armored Division. Battle groups of German tanks and infantry were in front of and behind Moyon. Our advance found one of these battle groups as we closed in on our objective south of the village. Two newly assigned lieutenants and the scouts of the two leading companies went down in the first spurt of machine gun fire. The Stonewall Brigade's three battalions deployed along the line of opposition; again we grappled with the enemy, and, whatever individual reluctance might have existed, corporately, we would not let go.

That night, the Luftwaffe mustered a lone plane to drone along the front, dropping flares whose white glare created a feeling of unwholesome exposure. Intermittent shelling continued the next morning. In the midst of it, we were ordered to send a company to a crossroads, called La Denisière, to the rear of our right flank, where there was an uncertain report of a roadblock of German tanks. G Company was given the mission, and around that inconspicuous crossing of dusty Norman roads waged one of those small bloody battles that thunder for those in them, but hardly a whisper in history.

The day, 30 July, also left its mark on me; late in its afternoon, I received word that the battalion commander had been hit in the forearm and was being evacuated. I was to take command. My first sensation was one of such complete inadequacy that it seemed important to share it with the regimental commander. I took a jeep back to his command post and advised him that there were undoubtedly officers standing around better-qualified for the job. The colonel did not dispute this but told me that I had accepted the promotion to executive officer, and I would now go back and command the battalion. My reluctance, however, must have raised doubt as to my qualities of leadership, for that evening he sent up a senior captain from his staff as executive officer and potential replacement.

So, I shouldered what seemed the full weight of the war, going first to La Denisière, where G Company had gained control of the crossroads. A German halftrack, its radio still crackling Teutonic military jargon, was tilted into a ditch, the bodies of the crew strewn about. The crossroads lay across the route of a new division being committed to Cobra, and the German command thought enough of its tactical value to waste four of their Mark IV tanks, as well as the halftrack, trying to block it. G Company had paid the price: Lying near the halftrack was a lieutenant who had joined the week before, unconscious and breathing with the heavy snoring sound characteristic of head wounds. Other still forms were collected in the shade of a hedgerow.

The day's cost did not end with G Company; the F Company commander and a newly joined lieutenant from H Company were also killed; the wounded and the emotional casualties amounted to another squad or so. Lieutenant Eugene M. Raggett, the dead company commander, was a young lawyer from California who—like Bob Hargrove, so badly wounded at Sainte-Claire—had chosen the infantry though he had entry into the Judge Advocate Corps. Add the loss of the battalion commander, and the toll for our fifteen miles of the pursuit was mounting, and we had hardly started.

That night, the German flare plane was accompanied by a bomber but disturbed nothing in the 2d Battalion except rest. With this second appearance, the flare plane naturally acquired the title of "Bed Check Charlie."

The next day was spent in place. Through the morning, seven panzers probed across our front, then suddenly turned and began blasting the hedgerows held by E Company. The company claimed disabling bazooka hits on one, which was towed away by the others. Later, a young German officer in the black panzer uniform was brought into the command post, his lower jaw a bloody mess of smashed teeth, bone, and flesh. He was on his feet but could make only gurgling noises and hold his head in obviously harrowing pain. Compassion for an enemy, I found, diminishes as a battle drags on—in Europe it was to reach its nadir in the misery of the Ardennes

— but enough remained that day to send this one back to the aid station by jeep.

Patrols that night found the Germans gone — the reason being, though we did not know it, that VIII Corps, on the right flank of Cobra, was breaking through the German defenses at the coastal town of Avranches. Through this corridor, the U.S. Third Army was to sweep westward into Brittany and eastward to form the southern side of the Argentan–Falaise pocket.

The effect of victory at Avranches was immediate: A pullback of German tank and infantry groups began all across the front. A departing army takes menace with it, leaving a palpable void. Into this void, the 2d Battalion advanced the next morning, finding no evidence of the enemy except for wrecked vehicles and freshly mounded roadside graves; in retreat, the Germans buried their dead as they went along. The great pursuit, though we did not think of it by title, was on. The 2d Battalion's line of advance lay across country, through summer fields and orchards in full fruit, and at times along country lanes marked by tank tracks that posed the continuing question of where they might stop. They did not stop that day, and we covered over two uneventful miles, digging in at dusk and hugging the shadows of hedgerows as Bed Check Charlie came over on his nightly swing.

The day had been a rare one of no casualties. My most anxious moments had come on seeing a rifle company trudging in file across the enemy side of a grassy slope, resembling moving targets in a shooting gallery. Company commanders' careers in Normandy were apt to be brief, allowing little chance to accumulate experience. This particular tactical rashness was not called to account by the German rear guard.

The next morning, we started again over the rolling hills and, in a wide swale, passed the debris of a tank battle. The scorched hulks of three Shermans and two Mark IVs were tumbled about, guns tilted at odd angles. A blackened body lay halfway out of the driver's hatch of a Sherman, arms extended and fingers crooked, clawing for escape. The passing files barely glanced at the scene; even the most morbid curiosity among us must have been long since satisfied.

That afternoon, the enemy became more active, adding to their delaying force a large-caliber, long-range mortar that lobbed its huge shells in at odd

116

intervals to avoid being located by our airborne artillery spotter. The mortar immediately established itself as a dreaded thing, its shells able to blow apart everything in a field. One of the first rounds did this to a squad and further dampened any exhilaration of the chase.

The battalion pushed on late into the soft evening of that day and started again the next morning through a white ground mist. Along the way, stray German soldiers, who had hidden out when their units retreated, came out of holes or houses and surrendered. They supplied little useful information, being too anxious to tell what they thought we wanted to hear about the sad straits of the German army and their personal anti-Nazi sentiments.

Also uncovered was a young American paratrooper who had been captured on D-day and had escaped to hide out with a farm family. He wore the beret and faded blue work clothes of the French farmer but remained unmistakably American to more than a glance.

Signs of the retreat abounded, but all the weapons and equipment we passed were smashed; there was none of the litter or usable materiél that trails a routed army. A farm, where we paused briefly, had been a depot for bicycle troops, and dozens of the heavy, cumbersome machines in various stages of repair were ranked in the barn and sheds. We admired much of the German equipment: their lower-slung tanks made Shermans appear awkwardly high and vulnerable; their P-38 pistol was much sought-after; their machine pistols and machine guns had a higher cyclic rate of fire than our Brownings had and seemed more deadly. I do not think, however, that any of our lads considered bicycles a desirable way to war, or practical as a souvenir, so they were left undisturbed. Some were probably repaired by the thrifty Norman farmers and are still in use.

The Stonewall Brigade's zone of advance now centered on the town of Vire, which we found, in due time, to be on the eastern side of a deep ravine cut through the hills by the Vire River. Vire, like Saint-Lô, is a road and market center, its origins dating back into the Middle Ages. Also like Saint-Lô, the hills and ridges around it are adapted for defense, and the nearer we drew, the harder and more costly became the going.

Third August was a day of brief encounters with delaying parties that ripped off bursts of automatic fire and then withdrew as our counterfire built up. Just when this withdrawal took place, and where it would stop again, was always a matter to explore carefully; it made for a slow advance.

Later that afternoon, near the village of Landelles-et-Coupigny, a heavier than usual volume of artillery, mortar, and tank fire exploded across the front, and we went to ground. Our artillery blasted back, and the stained stretchers were carried to the rear with their loads. So reminiscent was this of the approaches to Saint-Lô that I was convinced the rest of the way to Vire would be equally costly. This outlook grew darker with the evening until it developed into genuine gloom, a not unfamiliar emotion for me in the manic-depressive atmosphere of war. I was usually able to dissemble it and knew that I would have to come to grips with it now. I had seen soldiers led forward by desperation, but I had never seen them follow gloom in any direction other than to the rear.

Even the small forward command post group — all steady veterans — was too much company for this mood, so, with the radio operator, I went forward through the gloaming to a front-line hedgerow where a sparse squad of riflemen was dug in, resting or watching. Similar squads were in the fields to either flank, but so compartmented by the hedgerows that each had reason to feel alone in the war. The evening had grown quiet except for the far-off rumble of heavy traffic to the north and east as German armor and trucks pulled back from the developing pincer arms. Now and then, the rumble was interrupted by the dull crash and dim-red glow of shell fire as our artillery sought out the retreat. I stood for a few minutes watching this and the landscape just ahead, hazily lighted by some small phase of the moon. Then, on impulse, I told the radio operator to stay behind while I went up to the next hedgerow. He did not protest, nor did the squad leader, who saw no reason to object to a gratuitous outpost. After arranging signals to call me back and for me to announce my return, I clambered over the hedgerow and crossed the narrow field to the front.

Here, indeed, was the rare solitude that I think can be found only in the dead space between two resting armies. It could be violated by patrols, but this was unlikely considering the German posture of retreat. I felt no fear of disturbance as I leaned into the rank growth of the chest-high hedgerow and tried to think melancholy away. There was no military reason for it: We were winning the war. The 2d Battalion was a responsive command, becoming more effective by the day as the new men turned veteran. Making decisions involving lives was a heavy burden, but it was now an accustomed one, and less a moral weight in that my hide was also at stake — there is little impersonal decision-making in an infantry battalion. Then, too, these choices were largely dictated by what we were ordered to do. For tomorrow, the order was to attack at 0530, following a fifteen-minute artillery preparation. The riflemen would then maneuver forward, and, if the Germans had not pulled out, some would be killed and more wounded. To this relentless process of destruction, we were committed by discipline, pride, and, I think, by a still-abiding conviction that for Americans in 1944 there was no alternative.

It was while I was groping in this dark maze of the mind that a dimly perceived movement materialized on the opposite side of the hedgerow to the left. To present as fiction the scene that then developed would require only ordinary imagination; to claim it as fact would be absurd. I offer it as a particularly vivid hallucination from fatigue long-sustained, and the effect of continuing violence on an essentially nonviolent nature. The record of the war shows stranger things imagined in higher places, in less menacing surroundings, and passing at the time as cool reasoning. Not being attuned to the occult, or to more than mild, everyday hallucination, I can put no missionary zeal into describing it.

The scene that came into dim focus was a German patrol moving in my direction. This, in itself, would have been a sufficient shock; compounding it was a developing awareness that this patrol was not exactly of the Wehrmacht with which we had been in deadly embrace for the past two months, and its movement was as noiseless as the gathering of white ground fog in a low swale before me.

All of this was registered under the impact of imagined proximity to an enemy whom I never regarded with detachment at any range. The identification that developed in more detail was with the sepia-toned pictures of the Kaiser's army in an illustrated history of the Great War that I had pored over as boy. Soldiers of the Kaiser's Imperial Army and those of Hitler's Third Reich both wore helmets described as "coal scuttles" for their resemblance to a household implement of the era of the coal-burning stove. There were marked differences, however, between the cloth fatigue caps worn in the two wars. The cap of Hitler's army had a long bill and low crown, while the one the Kaiser's soldiers wore was round, high-standing, and had no visor at all — looking like a modified chef's bonnet but distinctively German. Each member of the patrol that I eventually made out wore the round cap of the Kaiser's army.

Further, each appeared to be shod in calf-high jackboots, which were universal in pictures of the World War I German army. Jackboots were also favored in this war, but I had noted that most of the prisoners we had been taking wore heavy shoes and short canvas gaiters.

Finally, at the time, I was convinced that at least every other German in my war was armed with the machine pistol whose tearing bursts were a more familiar sound than were single rifle shots. Rear guards and patrols favored the machine pistol, and I do not recall encountering one not so armed. But this patrol carried only rifles, the barrels slanting alternately right and left.

Old men do indeed forget; memories merge, shift, and take on none such shapes. So strong, however, was the impact of the antique figures and the aura they projected that they have remained with me intact down the years. It was a hallucination of uncommon power and shock effect.

I have said that the inky figures (there were six or eight of them) materialized suddenly and silently in space that had been empty. Countering an immediate imperative to leave their presence was the certainty that before I had lumbered a few yards, those rifles could be leveled for execution as if I were a condemned man tied to a stake. I do not recall considering my service automatic adequate to the odds. My uncalculated response was to crouch to eye-level with the top of the hedgerow and stare through the rank growth at the darker figures moving toward me in the night, only their upper bodies and rifles visible to me. Seconds more, and they would have been abreast. But then, without signal that I discerned, they stopped and bent below the level of the hedgerow, out of my vision.

One can withhold breathing for an eternity, for it was that long and I did, before the dark battle frieze again materialized above the hedgerow. But now, instead of continuing toward me, they turned hard left in single file, and in a predatory crouch moved the short distance into the obscurity filling the swale. They waded rapidly into the fog to become ebony blobs on its white surface and then to disappear. The turn had brought each figure into full-length silhouette, and I got the full effect of the caps, the rifles, and the jackboots that moved without a whisper through the grass.

Thus the hallucination passed. Gradually, I became aware again of the distant rumble of the retreat and of the summer rustlings and green smells of the hedgerow. The Impressionist landscape to my front, with the coal-black line of the next hedgerow drawn across it and the lighter splash of ground fog down its center, again held mystery more haunting than menacing. I do not know how long I stood so, and it was without conscious decision that I turned back across the narrow field to our lines, tapping the return signal on my helmet, probably unnecessarily because the sentries and the radio operator must have been able to make me out dimly the entire time.

No comments were made as I rejoined them, and self-preservation as a commander argued against mentioning that a German patrol from another war had passed by a field away. Too, I had been vehement about reports of enemy sightings and no action taken. My pronouncement that we could not hope to win the war and return home by just looking at the enemy had, I thought, a fine realistic ring. On looking back, I doubt that it did more than lessen the reports of sightings, for there is an unwritten soldiers' maxim: If you shoot at the enemy, he is likely to shoot back, and, therefore, it is an action that requires a fine calculation of the odds. I had a natural reluctance to reveal that I had just opted for the soldiers' adage over my own.

The radio operator and I returned to the command post where, except for the telephone watch, all were asleep along the hedgerow. The night had the hazy, dreamlike aspect of the glade scene in *A Midsummer Night's Dream*, but here, a different sort of human folly was afoot. I was aware, though, that my burden of gloom had lifted, and — lacking another reason — I attribute it to the shock of seeing a sight that never was. None of this says much for my emotional steadfastness, but that is not a point I am trying to establish. Wrapped in a slicker against the dew, I slept.

We were up in the dawn mist, each eating whatever part of the cold field-ration he could tolerate. The artillery preparation came in on time, and then the move forward. But here, the script departed from the one I had broodingly foreseen. The Germans had again pulled out, except for a few stragglers who were waiting to surrender.

Now, we were pointed straight for Vire, but across the path loomed Hill 219 dominating the western approaches. We had advanced little more than a mile when the enormously destructive shells from the heavy mortar, and artillery fire, exploded along the route. More men went down, and the companies dispersed along the hedgerows. The fire subsided but descended again each time we came under observation from the hill. Early in the evening, we dug in, and the 3d Battalion advanced through our positions for an attack on the hill the next morning. The evening was quiet except for tank gun fire off to the left front, where the 2d Armored was battling for a bridge over the river.

The next day, 5 August, was also costly. The 3d Battalion attacked, along with 2d Armored's tanks, and gained the left half of the hill. Early in the evening, we were ordered up on the right side and reached the broad, flat top just at dusk. A thin line was organized among the tanks already deployed along the eastern edge, overlooking the deep, dark ravine of the Vire River and the town on the opposite side. Now and again, an ear-splitting exchange of high-velocity tank gun fire cracked across the ravine.

The command post was in an ancient barn that held the penetrating smell of musty hay, animals, and untold generations of mice. The seriously wounded were sent down the rough hillside by stretcher, and the lesser-hurt were collected in the barn for the night. A young soldier, with what must have been a painful flesh wound, assured me that he was all right as an aid man injected a Syrette of morphine and had him take sulfa tablets against infection. It was widely observed that American wounded rarely cried out in that war, though there was enough pain to raise a cry to heaven. It was an army that rarely sang in ranks or yelled in battle. It was followed by the "quiet generation" of the 1950s, and then, in complete reversal, by the raucous generation of the 1960s — an ebb and flow of decibels that is no doubt part of the cyclic nature of things.

We remained on the hill throughout the morning and afternoon of 6 August, dug in against the artillery and tank fire that broke out intermittently. Late in the afternoon, the tankers, after private communication among themselves, abruptly cranked up and roared away without so much as a wave. The 2d and 3d battalions were now the sole and battered kings of 219. Shortly thereafter came a warning order to prepare to assault Vire.

I had spent the day at the forward edge of the hill, where there was a clear view of the town on the opposite and slightly lower height. From here, it looked like a picture postcard, the backs of the closely set houses, with red tile roofs, making a varicolored wall above the steep valley. Vire was acquainted with calamity: It had known terrible passages of the Black Death in the fourteenth century, innumerable local conflicts of feudal lords, and, in the fifteenth century, the devastation of the Hundred Years War. Its most recent disaster had been a D-day air raid that wrecked it and left many of its citizens dead or injured. Now, two months later, on a beautiful August evening of the mid-twentieth century, its ancient stones were to be again tumbled about, this time in a contention between the Stonewall Brigade, sometime of the Army of Northern Virginia, Confederate States of America, and a conglomerate of German paratroops, infantry, and armor. It was, I suppose, an incident of history neither more nor less likely than any other. As probably happened in its ancient calamities, the more resourceful and wary inhabitants had fled, the less wary lay buried in the rubble.

I had not expected the attack order. The ravine and river, I thought, must be recognized as too formidable an obstacle for our depleted ranks. It seemed logical that we invest the town, and the attack be made in greater strength along some less-precipitous approach. This wishful logic was voided by the arrival of Colonel Dwyer with word that in just over two hours the 2d and 3d battalions were to take Vire and block the five roads converging there.

In giving this order to Bill Puntenney, commanding the 3d, and to me, he was not quite able to conceal his apprehension over the prospect. A big, heavyset man, he was having a difficult time pleasing the divisional commander who was his opposite in stature and temperament. The clash building between the two already pointed to his departure. Both dealt with my shortcomings with considerable forbearance, and I have reason to be grateful to both; on the differences between them, I am unable to pass judgment.

The general kept tabs on his three regiments by posting liaison officers to each regimental commander to report developments directly to him

123

without waiting for the slower staff channels. The young lieutenant posted to the 116th was a bumbling type, and in his zeal to hear what was being told Puntenney and me, he stumbled and fell against the colonel — sending his map board with its overlays spinning. This would not have been excused under any circumstance. Now, given the colonel's anxiety over the mission and probably resentment of what he considered the general's snooping, he delivered a monumental bawling-out that left the lieutenant riddled. It also served to relieve the dark prospects of the attack — a moment of relief in a somber play. While the rest of us brought coughing under control, the colonel straightened out his rumpled dignity and, apparently feeling better, laid out the battalion boundaries and objectives. Then, with a blessing of "good luck, and don't fail," he departed with a final admonishment to keep him informed.

I went over the order with the company commanders and, in turn, assigned boundaries and objectives, which they accepted without expressed misgivings. Then, there was a surprise call on the field telephone, from the general, asking how long I had had to prepare for the attack. He actually sounded a little uncertain, and I found myself foolishly trying to reassure probably one of the most assured men in the army that all would be well.

By now, evening shadows were stretching out, leaving our west side of the ravine dark and highlighting the opposite side. Vire appeared in this light as a medieval town under siege, black smoke rising above it and artillery fire echoing along the defile. A short stretch of the road entering the town from the southwest was visible, and on this a squat German tank lurched into view, traversed its gun, and began pumping shells down the ravine at a target we could not see, possibly the river bridge. John Hodges, the artillery observer, registered the fire of a battery on it, the first shell hitting directly in front of the turret in a spasm of flame. Through field glasses, I saw the tank rock like a poleaxed steer, its tracks shedding dust and its gun silenced; then, slowly, it crawled out of view toward the town, followed by more shell splashes. So, we knew there was at least one tank in Vire, the crew counting themselves lucky at its having been hit by a high explosive rather than an armor-piercing shell.

The two assault companies started in columns abreast down the steep hillside and were immediately lost to view in the underbrush and dark shadows. The battalion command group followed, slipping and sliding, holding onto brush and trees. At the bottom, we passed one of the first wounded, a rifleman, bandaged and lying beside the river. He raised on an elbow and asked to be helped back to the aid station. I had to tell him that no one of our small party could be spared, but that the stretcher bearers with the reserve company were following directly behind and would take care of him. He sank back without complaint; a recurring and troubling wonder is whether he was found in the fading light.

We forded the shallow river and started up the opposite slope toward a racket of gunfire beyond the wall of houses. Stragglers were drifting back toward the river, each announcing himself to be the sole survivor of his squad or platoon. They were pressed into our party, and we entered the town through a narrow lane that opened between the houses. The scene inside was worthy of a witches' sabbath: the night lit by the undulating red glow of burning buildings, all overhung by a pall of smoke. The only orgy under way, however, was that of destruction: Parties of Germans were trying to surrender; others were trying to withdraw and doing a lot of yelling and screaming; tracer bullets crisscrossed and ricocheted off the rubble. In the general madness and confusion, some who had surrendered undoubtedly changed their minds and slipped away.

The two assault companies had dissolved in the debris, and the only usable force still in hand was the reserve company that pushed along the main street to the eastern exit of the town. On this street was a massive, two-storied stone building, and here the command group stopped and tried to get the battalion into some sort of order. We had no contact with regiment either by wire or radio. Two company commanders were casualties, as was the battalion executive officer, who had been loyal and energetic in helping me though he was undoubtedly ambitious for command. I understood this; it was the crazy unfathomable chance of war that it was he, and not I, who was wounded.

The night finally grew quiet, and with what seemed undue reluctance gave way to a dawn milky with ground mist. Vire by daylight lost the dramatic appearance it had had by firelight the night before and became just another dismal place of gray, smoking rubble. What was left of the battalion was pulled into a tighter perimeter, blocking the roads. The principal block was farther along the street from the command post and centered on a heavy machine gun of H Company set up on the edge of a bomb crater. I was talking to the crew about the field of fire when, directly to the front and at no more than fifty yards' distance, a close column of troops debouched onto the road from a wooded area, turning away from us, eastward. While it was reasonably certain that they were not American, in the haze of fatigue and visibility, I hesitated to order fire upon what was the gruesome ideal of a machine gun target: the long axis of the marching column lying directly in the long axis of the gun's cone of fire. By the time I had concluded that it was an enemy column, and the gunner had touched off a burst, it was vanishing down a slope into the mist, much luckier than it deserved to be. At the time, I blamed myself for the lost opportunity to destroy some whose purpose — probably achieved to some degree — was to destroy us. Now, forty-five years later, I can hope that some of them survived the war.

Returning to the command post, I found the wounded gathered into the cobbled courtyard with only the limited help a company aid man could give them. While I was still boiling over the slowness of our battalion aid station, a German paratrooper surgeon and his crew of aid men were brought in as POWs, and I asked him to give emergency care to our injured. He agreed, and, with the efficiency of long practice, he and his crew cleared a table in a bright room and set out bandages and instruments from their field medical kits. With assembly-line precision, a dozen or more of our wounded were stanched, cleaned, and bandaged. Along with everything else I had seen of the front-line German soldier, this work was professional and competent. I was glad that there were not more of them.

Our best battalion surgeon was a young doctor from Puerto Rico, Jorge Herter, who was a cheerful and steadfast asset to the battalion from the time he was assigned soon after Vire until the end of the war. It was not long before the men dubbed him Doc Herter. I formulated the field rule that any surgeon or aid man known to his outfit by the informal title "Doc" was a good one.

It was now midmorning. There had been quiet since dawn, but now a shell from our old enemy, the heavy mortar, slammed into one end of the building, followed by a salvo of artillery fire that stirred and pulverized the rubble once again. The explosions continued walking through the ruins at intervals. The German surgeon called attention to his rights as a POW to be moved from the danger zone, and, during a lull in the shelling, he was sent to the rear with the wounded.

Late that afternoon, Colonel Dwyer again arrived with an order. This time, it was to take Hill 251, which loomed over Vire to the east and was probably the observation post for the shelling. The 1st Battalion was to take a similar hill to the south. A battalion of the 2d Infantry Division arrived to take over Vire, and we advanced to the base of the hill for the attack the next morning, 7 August.

The afternoon's advance uncovered a German rifleman who had sniped several Stonewallers during the day: He waited too long to pull out and was cut down on the run down a narrow garden lane. The night at the foot of the hill was quiet, the German artillery continuing to rend the town, now to our rear.

Preparation for the attack was automatic: One rifle company — now about fifty men — and the heavy weapons would form a firebase on the right, while the other two companies — with a combined strength of less than one — attacked on the left along a farm road. The morning mist cleared by jump-off time at 0630, and the hill's great round shape reared above us in the light of another bright August day. The artillery preparation, and our firebase, opened on the moment and soon created their own haze around the crest. The two assault companies started up and had not gone far before tearing bursts of machine gun fire started clipping the hedge tops. Among the first casualties was an Indian from the Southwest, naturally called Chief, who had been at the front of every attack starting with D-day. I had tried to talk to him as one of the remaining veterans but got only monosyllables in answer. What his thoughts were in fighting at the front of what was essentially white America's war, I was unable to determine. Now, he stumbled down the slope blinded by blood streaming from a deep scalp wound. He did not return to the regiment and became another of the hundreds who shed blood in its ranks and then disappeared. There is a latter-day wonder at what turn his memories take: nostalgia for the brief admiration that his courage gained, or anger at having spent it so?

After this show of opposition, the defenders pulled out, and the attack went up with a rush to find the hill's broad top compartmented into fields and orchards. The riflemen coalesced along the hedgerows fencing in a red brick farmhouse; inside were a number of enemy wounded left behind — something that had not happened before. Suddenly, from a field or so beyond the house, came sounds of a loud argument in German, apparently between those who wanted to surrender and others who wanted to retreat and shoot at us another day. More artillery fire was called in to encourage surrender, and one of our men promoted the idea in Milwaukee dialect. It seemed that every outfit had in its ranks some who spoke a version of German passed down from immigrant forefathers. French-speaking soldiers were not so plentiful; ours was a lanky Cajun whose French seemed to puzzle the Normans and whose English sometimes stumped me.

Apparently, the diehards among the arguing enemy prevailed, for the loud voices faded. The communications platoon labored up with the latest extension of a telephone line that they had started laying on Omaha Beach two months before. I got through to Colonel Dwyer to tell him that the objective was taken, and he sounded surprised and relieved. There is a flamboyant battlefield tradition that on such occasions one announces that his command awaits further orders. Not wanting further orders, I ignored this tradition.

The firebase company and the heavy weapons crews came up and a defensive was set up around our holdings. Checking around the perimeter, I stopped at an outpost that looked across another ravine to Hill 203, taken by the 1st Battalion that morning in a skillfully conducted action that won for it a Presidential Citation. A stretch of farm lane along the bottom of the ravine was in view, and, as we watched, three or four Germans appeared, trudging along it in single file, apparently in retreat from Hill 203. Very much as in a shooting gallery, one of our riflemen crumpled them into gray bundles. Presently, another figure appeared on the lane, as from offstage, waving a large Red Cross flag. He examined the bundles, and apparently finding them lifeless, exited slowly into the wings still waving his flag. The rifleman who had done the shooting had a wolfish grin; the rest looked on without speaking. There were few avid killers in our ranks.

I continued on around the perimeter and, toward its northern part, followed a high stone wall that ended at the side of a farm building. Laboring along this wall, vastly weary, I became aware of thumping sounds behind me, and, just before I reached the building, there was a louder thump in front and stone chips flew from the impact of a bullet. Only then did it dawn that I was being tracked by a distant sniper; the next shot would likely be on target. The only exit from the situation was through an open window directly in front of me in the side of the building, the sill about shoulder-high. Without conscious thought and from a standing start, I dove through into shelter — the outstanding athletic achievement of my life, and not a mean one by any standard. A sergeant and some riflemen in the room where I landed in a heap were apparently beyond surprise, for they did not comment on this unorthodox entrance of the battalion commander. I cautioned them about the sniper and left by the other end of the building, following the protected side of the wall down to the command post on the western slope of the hill.

It was still early afternoon. I was certain that we had reached a stopping point, that nothing more could be asked of the now truly decimated 2d Battalion other than to hold where it was. With this comforting conviction — for which there was no basis in experience — I lay down in the cool grass and drifted into a half-doze. This pleasant state did not last long: Sharp explosions of M-1 rifle fire from the top of the hill brought me up with a start and set the field phone buzzing. In a few moments, word came down that two German motorcycles with sidecars had been driven into our lines and had been promptly bushwhacked. Shortly afterward, four POWs were marched into the command post, carrying a young staff captain who was wounded in the foot. The captain looked the part of a German war poster: handsome, blond, and tall. He and his party had evidently been on reconnaissance and unaware that the hill was no longer German-held. As I have noted, this happened often enough on both sides to constitute the prime hazard to staff service.

While the intelligence officer (S-2) was collecting material from the motorcycles, I offered the captain a field-ration and we talked about the war, he speaking heavily accented, but adequate, English. I handed him one of the leaflets, which had been showered on the Germans, pointing out the hopelessness of their situation and urging surrender. He said, pleasantly enough, that it was foolish to expect an army that had fought as the German army had fought for the past five years to surrender to such pieces of paper. I observed that as far as he was concerned, this was academic. He agreed but advised me not to expect the German army to fall apart. He complimented the field-ration, and I said that if he found that palatable, his army was in worse shape than he realized.

The conversation was drifting into banter as the S-2 arrived with maps and papers from the sidecars. The captain looked at the bundle ruefully as he was carried away by the other POWs on a stretcher improvised from a door. I cautioned him of the practice of our rear-area people of stripping POWs of watches, medals, and anything else removable. He said that German rear-area troops did the same and that I should get the good Luger pistol that had been taken from him. It would have been hard to have wished so pleasant a fellow reduced to another lifeless heap on a dusty Norman hilltop. One of the motorcycles was undamaged, and I used it for a few days until regiment heard about it and ordered it turned in.

The rest of the day and night were quiet. The next morning, 9 August, patrols found no sign of the enemy other than fresh graves and wrecked equipment. We did not know that two days before, some fifteen miles to the southwest, the last German offensive in Normandy had been launched to sever the breakthrough corridor at Avranches, through which the U.S. Third Army was rolling. This futile effort was drawing all their resources.

The battalion that had relieved us at Vire now took over Hill 251, and we marched back to join the rest of the regiment in corps reserve in an area southwest of the town, the battalion on the march looking like one full-strength company. There was a hot supper waiting, and the next day clean uniforms were issued to replace those we had sweated, fought, and slept in for the past ten days. Current editions of the *Stars and Stripes* arrived and told of a booming Allied war effort. The German counterattack had been stopped at Mortain after hard fighting, with never a pause in the Third Army columns that were pouring into Brittany and also curving in toward Falaise.

New men arrived to bring the companies up to over half-strength, and training was resumed. A white-haired lieutenant colonel from a replacement depot also came by, saying, very businesslike, that he wanted to observe at first hand the "maintenance job" on the battalion. I am sure that he meant well and was dedicated to his job of fairly allocating badly strained infantry manpower. The inference, however, that those we had left along the road to Vire, so many of whom I knew so well, were simply broken or worn-out parts to be replaced by new parts struck me as intolerable. My unfortunate tendency to sputter incoherently when angry surfaced to the astonishment of the well-meaning officer, who must have left thinking that his maintenance work would soon have to include a new battalion commander. If, however, he reported this unmannerly reaction to his innocent usage, it was never mentioned.

During these few days in bivouac, we were visited by General Gerhardt, and there was a formation at which he presented the Purple Hearts and Bronze Stars that had accumulated. All visitors told us that we had done well, and I do not recall any disclaimers.

There had been losses in all ranks, and reorganization was constant. Faircloth, senior captain, was made executive officer, only to be killed the following month at Brest. Captain Si Johnson, the new operations officer (S-3), the fourth in two months, arrived and was to prove a mainstay and a friend. We were both wounded the same day near Aachen, he losing his leg but never his warm and generous nature. The surviving lieutenants became company commanders, and Bob Garcia, who had been wounded at the Elle River crossing, returned from hospital to take over E Company again. Newly assigned lieutenants seemed to be mostly from Texas A&M University.

Such a litany of change runs through any account of infantry warfare. It is remarkable that with it the battalion's character remained so constant. The reason must be that despite all the arrivals and departures, enough of the past always remained to provide continuity. New men tended to regard the veterans with respect and adopted their attitudes and actions. Thus, even a relatively few veterans remaining in a battle-worthy battalion had great influence in keeping it so; by the same token, a hard-luck outfit with a background of failure was very hard to turn around.

The third day in reserve ended in a spurt of activity as we were ordered back to Hill 251, some higher echelon having decided that the Germans might turn and strike at Vire as they had at Avranches. This proved a far-fetched concern that might better have been saved for the Ardennes situation four months hence. Some of the veterans, however, pointed out that being deployed had its advantages, for had we stayed in bivouac we would have been doing close-order drill.

The battalion marched back to the hill that evening and was dug in by midnight, ready for a counterattack that became more remote by the day. Training was resumed in the form of rerunning the attack on the hill. Doubtlessly, the tactics were embellished with the practice, and each veteran probably gilded his part a bit, also. I did not reenact my leap through the window. The new men seemed impressed and intent on learning from so recent an action.

Meanwhile, the war rolled eastward, taking along Glory, its fancy lady, who has never been any better than she should be. Little of the German Seventh Army escaped; their Fifteenth Army was near rout in Flanders; the Parisians rose against their occupiers; the Allied invasion of southern France gained momentum. For the 2d Battalion, I think, this was all one; our small, violent scene on the giant canvas of the pursuit was done; we were in no rush to start on another.

5

Siege of Brest

"I'm told it's stunning when a battle's going badly, as even the best behaved battles will do at times, . . . and the authorities want to bring about a decision."

"This sounds interesting!"

"I'm glad you think so."

"And you know this recipe?"

"Yes; this is it — follow me closely. . . . You hurl yourself into the enemy ranks . . ."

"Yes."

"You're following me?"

"Closely, closely."

"And you let — " Jerphanion paused with carefully calculated effect — "cold steel decide!"

"Cold steel! Why, of course!" exclaimed Fabre with the ecstatic air of one who has seen the light. "Of course!"

They decided forthwith that the moment was ripe for a "thirty seconds' burst of continuous laughter." This was one of the more recently invented parts of the ritual.

Verdun, Jules Romains
(Alfred A. Knopf, Inc., 1939)

For the better part of a week, the 29th rested in the wake of the departed battle and in the heady prospect of a winding-down war. British-Canadian divisions, forming the northern arm of the pincer around the Argentan–Falaise pocket, pinched out our sector of the front, and even the sounds of war faded.

Late one afternoon, a British armored car troop pulled into bivouac in front of the 2d Battalion. I walked up to meet the commander and to find out what he knew about the war. I found him to be a beefy, walrus-moustached captain, stretched out in the shade of his car, which looked like an oversize jeep with a superstructure of light armor plate. One of his troopers was parading about nearby in a top hat and tail coat that must have belonged to the mayor of a Norman village.

The captain's conversational effort consisted of half-swallowed "hmms" and other even more unintelligible sounds. To my eye, the outfit had not been very hard-used, or even up to serious business, for the thin armor plate of its cars would hardly stop a .30-caliber rifle bullet. I came away feeling that these people would not have fared well under "Uncle Charlie" Gerhardt.

An infantry division in an active theater does not remain long unemployed. We had six days of basking in fine weather (the August of 1914 exactly thirty years before had also held fair for the Allied and German armies killing and maiming each other down toward a turn of war on the Marne). Then, the field phones began their muted ring, and smudged copies of mimeographed operational orders flowed downward.

The upshot was that early on the morning of 22 August the Stonewall Brigade — along with the rest of the 29th — loaded onto two-and-a-half-ton trucks, and again it was "Ho! and to the wars!" — one of those unbelievably foolish catch phrases developed long ago and surely far from any battle front. Uttered at Vire in August 1944, it would have drawn looks of amazement, followed by at least one of the "thirty seconds' bursts of continuous laughter" developed by Jerphanion and Fabre for such as "hurling oneself onto the enemy," and using "cold steel." Anyone using it would have had a short stay in the 2d Battalion.

The trucks were not foolish or flamboyant but were, along with the original jeep, simple, rugged workhorses. Inevitably, these qualities have since been diminished by the urge to make the simple complex, add refinements, and increase production profits: this, despite the so-often-repeated lessons that fortune in war favors only the simple in plan and execution; that complexity in maneuvers or matériel is invariably punished; and that gimmicky is run over roughshod, its presence hardly noticed.

The direction pointed by the march order was unexpected. Instead of eastward to the battle surging toward Germany, we were to head south and west to lay siege to the Breton port city of Brest. This assignment caused no dismay, as a report gained quick currency that the twenty thousand or so Germans isolated there in the backwash of the war were anxious to surrender to a proper show of force.

We should have known better. Each operation had started on such a high tide of hope—the manic phase of what I have said is war's manic-depressive emotional cast. Events had invariably dispelled this euphoric state in short order. Events at Brest did so again and revealed what might have been deduced at the start: that the German command was well aware that the now upward of two million Allied troops on the continent could not be supplied through the partially restored port of Cherbourg, a few Channel fishing ports, and the disintegrating artificial harbors on the D-day beaches. That the Seine River ports and those of the Breton peninsula were the answer to this problem was equally obvious to both sides. Holding these ports, the Germans held a logistical halter around the neck of the rearing and lunging Allied advance into their homeland. This halter would not be let go without a fight.

The Breton ports had been a major objective for the breakout from the beachhead but had been sidetracked in favor of the heady prospect of destroying the German armies in France and then advancing into Germany itself. Now, the supply situation dimmed this prospect and again focused attention on securing the ports; nor could the sizable garrison in Brest be ignored. It had either to be contained—requiring a large number of troops—or destroyed. The major German submarine base at Brest was also a magnet to draw Allied metal.

Brest was in the province of the U.S. VIII Army Corps. The decision being made to take the city, the 2d and 29th infantry divisions, two Ranger battalions, and additional artillery battalions were added to the corps' 8th Infantry Division, and the operation was put in train. Meanwhile, the German garrison was not preparing to yield to a show of force but to repel it. Nearer fifty thousand soldiers, sailors, marines, and airmen were available for this, rather than the twenty thousand estimated.

This is all afterview. On that 22 August, my strategic oversight of the war was obscured by the problems of the motor march, which developed into something of a triumphal progress through Brittany. There were not enough road maps of the route available, so the better part of a regiment was drawn on for guides, who were posted at critical turnings. Even this premium could not deny the infinite range of human error, a fact I encountered right at the start as my jeep came over a rise, and, at no more than a hundred yards' distance, I saw a dusty soldier at a crossroad pointing confidently for an eastward turning. I was following a smudged sketch-map and noted with instant apprehension that he seemed to be indicating the general direction of Paris, not Brittany.

Now that most of my life's turnings have been made, I can look back upon that one with some detachment, but I was not detached then; the prospect of leading a battalion of the 29th astray or of halting and upsetting a march schedule was a concern with which to conjure, though not for long, for we were within seconds of the necessity for a decision. I opted for the sketch-map and judgment, neither one a bible of direction, and with more hope than confidence led the long line of trucks in what proved to be the right direction.

Emotionally, the day brightened considerably after that and became compatible with the clear skies and warm summer air. The French national custom of taking August, en masse, for a vacation is deeply rooted, and, pursuant to custom, the roads fill annually with traffic and temper, especially those toward the sea. Not so this August 1944. War suspended custom, and our rumbling line of trucks rolled without hindrance over paved roads and dusty ones, making only the scheduled rest stops. Even soldiers not noted for delicacy of expression used this title for the halts to relieve bodily pressures. A line of troops standing attentively facing the roadside ditch at ten minutes of the hour is one of the images of the war.

A stance at the roadside ditch is also a custom of male travelers in France and apparently does not offend. Bretons waved and cheered and, at the stops, gathered to exchange food and drink for cigarettes. C-rations alone were not readily accepted in trade, the Bretons probably having been burned on this item when Third Army columns had gone through early on in Cobra. I did not try to curb the exercise of free trade, conducted through the universal language of barter, but it did add to the problem of keeping the column rolling on schedule. Concluding trades within the short period of a rest stop undoubtedly left some shortchanged, but in the atmosphere of general jubilation I do not believe this caused much anguish; both sides were abnormally generous.

General Gerhardt inspected the column on the march just before the noon break. He found the trucks spaced at his ordained interval, troops with helmet straps buckled, and no cigarettes visible — all of which was soothing to his formidable temper. In aid of this happy circumstance, I had just toured the column before him, correcting offenders with all the emphasis possible under the hazard of an open mouth in heavy dust. I had not thought, however, to caution drivers against accidentally shooting themselves in the leg, and this is just what one did during the lunch stop — probably the only shot he fired during the war, outside of the rifle range. The general had just bounded into his jeep and departed, which was fortunate, for he held commanders irrevocably responsible for such mishaps.

All in all, the motor march to Brest supplied additional support for my forthright claim to a Great Good Luck Medal, which I have said should be in the array authorized by the Republic to recognize a wide range of activities of its warriors. The Great Good Luck (something more original than a four-leaf clover and horseshoe should be in its design) would recognize those who were consistently, not just occasionally, favored by fortune above and beyond any they could possible deserve. It should take rank immediately after awards for valor and before the likes of the Good Conduct Medal and that for being on the same continent with the war. Making it an award for which one can only propose one's self would largely eliminate enlarged egos, and this would add luster.

Gook luck and all, the battalion closed into an assembly area about ten miles northwest of Brest that evening, thus ending a lighthearted prologue to a bloody play that, over the next three weeks of its run, would cost the 29th over two thousand casualties. With the onset of dusk, the day's aura of triumph departed and the ominous one of danger returned. Some 6th Armored Division people, who were investing the city, were nearby and assured us that we were not confronted by a cage of purring pussycats, anxious to please and surrender, but by tough soldiers ready to fight, including the 2d Parachute Division, intact in the town. The thinly scattered posts of the 6th Armored felt that they were containing on the sufferance of the contained, an understandably uncomfortable and lonely job.

An intelligence report said that Brest was commanded by a General Ramcke, whose 1st Parachute Division had exacted such a heavy price of the Allies at Monte Cassino, Italy, the previous winter. Evidently, he intended to do the same at Brest, and while he did not have the advantage of rugged mountain terrain to fortify his position, the lines around Brest were formidable enough: an outer ring of fieldworks dug in among the hedgerows; an inner ring keyed to a series of massive Napoleonic-era forts; and, finally, an ancient stone wall around the inner city. In all three rings were machine guns in concrete and steel emplacements protected by antitank ditches, minefields, and barbed wire. Three years of air raids had attracted a plentiful supply of antiaircraft guns that could bear in any direction and elevation.

To reduce these defenses and destroy those manning them, we had three veteran infantry divisions and the support of overwhelming sea and air power that, after the first two weeks, bombarded and bombed practically unopposed. Still another force worked against the besieged — silently, unremittingly, invisibly, and immeasurably — more defeating than the bombs and bullets. This force was an accumulating awareness by those in Brest that their only choices were death or surrender; there could be no victory or escape. Men have gone to epic death in the grip of fell circumstance: the French Foreign Legionnaires at Camerone, the Americans at the Alamo, and on and on. But, the spark that ignites the human spirit to death-defiant flame was not struck at Brest. Resistance there died with a relatively few fanatics; the mass became increasingly intent on surrendering and living. It seems that the death-stand of sagas is rarely made by masses, which are bound to contain a large proportion of spirits incapable of it. Masses caught in hopeless circumstances show more a tendency to stand submissively and be slaughtered than to fight. Defiance to the end is more in the province of the small, select band: The Legionnaires at Camerone numbered eighty-seven; the doomed garrison of the Alamo fewer than two hundred.

Nor were we, the besiegers, unaffected by the foregone conclusion of the end at Brest. Soldiers are understandably reluctant to die to accomplish sure victory, which, so far as we know, can be enjoyed only by the living. The spirit, I believe, did not sing on either side at the siege of Brest. It was a dun-gray business, conducted in generally warm, bright weather, cooled by coastal breezes.

By 25 August, the constricting lines about the city were in place and tightening of the screw began. The 29th, forming the right of the VIII Corps, started the attack with its regiments abreast. The 2d Battalion was in reserve of the 116th column, which was led by the 3d. Two nights later, the regiment was withdrawn from the center of the division's sector and moved to its right flank to open a new front astride a ridge line along which ran a main road into the city.

This time, 28 August, the 2d Battalion had the lead and began to bleed. Over the first three days of the siege, the regiment recorded twenty-three killed and ninety-two wounded; the toll for the next five days on the new front was 106 killed and 361 wounded, all spent against a stronghold dug in around the farm hamlet of La Trinité. It was the bloody type of hedgerow fighting that we had hoped had been left behind in Normandy. German artillery had not yet been silenced, and the La Trinité positions seemed impervious to our guns. The cost worried our superiors, as well it might; we had already a long enough casualty list, and no command wants the reputation of being an excessive bleeder. Nonetheless, La Trinité could not be bypassed if the siege lines were to constrict further.

The 1st and 2d battalions were given a day to prepare for a midnight attack. Some refresher practice was done at maintaining direction with compass, and with flank squads stringing white engineer tape to mark boundaries so that riflemen would not stray in the hedgerow maze, compounded by darkness. The night attack succeeded with surprising ease. The battering given the defenders had evidently taken a greater toll than we knew; our silent ally — hopelessness — must also have added its weight.

On the following afternoon, the most critical hours of the siege struck for the 2d Battalion as the Germans mounted a counterattack to retake La Trinité, the weight of it hitting G Company on our right flank. So deceptive are battle sounds that, at the command post a few fields away, I thought a sudden crash of German artillery preceding the counterattack was not hitting our sector at all, until an out-of-breath runner stumbled in with an urgent call from the company commander for reinforcement. By the time the reserve platoon arrived, it was all over. The field in front of the right G Company platoon was littered with bodies in paratrooper smocks and others in marine uniform. It was a profusion of death I had not seen in so small a place since the first day at Saint-Lô.

Immediate counterattack to regain a lost position is militarily sound, but this one was about eight hours late. Whoever ordered it without prior probing, little artillery preparation, and in a tactically foolish formation was either rash or acting in anger. I suspect the latter: La Trinité had been lost to the night attack without a hard fight, so punish those who had lost it by ordering a counterattack too late, and with too little means. Pity soldiers who have an angered commander who declares, "I don't care how many casualties it costs!" If there were immediate — as opposed to delayed — justice in war, the commander, at whatever level, uttering these words would have to lead the attack in person, a requirement that would calm anger, clear judgment, and save lives.

As conceived and implemented, the counterattack could only have succeeded if the G Company platoon had abjectly submitted, and this might have been the case had not Sergeant Wilson R. Carr roused it to fight. The shock and fury of close battle and encounter with death still on him, Sergeant Carr told me that after the sudden crash of artillery lifted, he had looked over the hedgerow and seen the crowd of paratroopers and marines coming across the field on the run, firing as they came. He had begun picking them off with his rifle — he was credited with fifteen — and shouting to his platoon to get up and fight or be killed. Enough joined him to wipe out the attackers. In the deathly quiet that followed, one of the wounded was seen to push up to a sitting position and with his pistol self-administer the *coup de grâce*.

After a lengthy study, an awards board found that Sergeant Carr's valor had saved a rupture of our lines, and all the blood and trouble that would have ensued. He was awarded the Distinguished Service Cross, the first for the battalion since three were won on D-day. Decorations for valor did not come cheaply in the 29th. In a year of nearly unbroken combat, and over twenty thousand casualties, the deeds of only two men — both sergeants

— were deemed worthy of the Medal of Honor; both were killed in action before their medals were approved.

The brief fight for relatively minute stakes in an ordinary hedge-enclosed field outside La Trinité, Brittany, on a cloudy August afternoon, 1944, was a microcosm of war at all times and levels. It encompassed misconception, chance, rashness, violence, courage, despair, victory, and defeat — all monitored by death. Clashes between nations hold no more, or no less.

It was representative, too, in that the outcome pivoted upon an individual. That war turns upon a man, and not upon men, is hardly an original observation, but it is generally applied to the head of state, or the commander at the stratospheric level. I found it equally applicable at the platoon and company level. There was no successful action of the 2d Battalion that was not made possible by one or two souls who burned for the moment at a white-hot flame. When these few did not emerge or were killed before their parts were played, there was failure. A researcher of the Omaha Beach assault decided, with I know not what degree of accuracy, that of all those engaged on the more than six miles of beach, the actions of no more than forty-seven turned the day from disaster to precarious success.

So it was with the Germans at Brest. As the will of the mass weakened, the fate of the ever-dwindling defiant few became more deadly. One such doom was decreed in the late afternoon, several days later, while I was with a company in a sunken lane, talking with the commander. All was quiet when, suddenly, potato-masher grenades came sailing over in salvos of six or eight, the range so misjudged that they cleared the lane and exploded behind us. Following the third or fourth flight of grenades, a young paratrooper leaped into the lane, landing just off the left flank of the company line. I have never forgotten that rather slight figure, in round helmet and camouflage smock, tense as a tightly coiled spring, whirling in surprise to face us, rifle at port. Those who were supposed to follow him did not; he dove for cover but never lived to reach it. I doubt that he received a posthumous Iron Cross, for those who failed to follow him would not have been likely to propose it and thus call attention to their own failure to act.

La Trinité was the most costly part of the siege for the 2d Battalion. The price included Captain Faircloth, who had been executive officer since the reorganization following Vire. He was killed while temporarily leading a rifle company that had lost its officers, and I felt it deeply. He was the type of soldier who inspires trust by his example of common sense, steadiness, and cheer. He was on the way back to his proper job as executive when he was killed; the memory of how much difference a few minutes would have made is painful.

Another on that lengthening list with Faircloth is Sergeant Alva L. Newton of E Company, one of the battalion's best athletes and a star in the intercompany football games back in England. A German shell came in on an angle that penetrated the few feet of hedgerow where he was dug in, and that was all. Also close to home was my runner, whom I had sent to locate a company commander. Evidently taking a wrong turn in the hedgerows, he walked into a German post. There were others — too many.

Now, the ring around Brest tightened; our artillery, air strikes, and naval bombardment steadily reduced the German artillery's power to retaliate. There was an apparent lack of German mortars in our sector, which was especially appreciated. Lessening of enemy-imposed battlefield discipline gave rise to carelessness and exacted a price. After some days of little or no shelling, some of our Headquarters Company people were caught by a sudden salvo of shells that tore into the house where they had gathered to heat rations. German observers must have been biding their time for such an opportunity. Some good men were killed; a sight that replayed in my memory is of a soldier holding his dying comrade in his arms and pleading that he live.

As the German situation obviously deteriorated, General Gerhardt thought it possible to end it by a raid to cut out and bring back General Ramcke. The raiding party was to go in by boat, rowed from our flank on the Bay of Brest to land behind the German flank. He called to tell me to plan to lead it; my response could best be described as choked. A short time later, Colonel Dwyer called and expressed misgivings with which I was able to relate instantly. Colonel Dwyer's objections prevailed, for I heard no more about the raid. It is a feat one could dream of having performed, but certainly not yearn to undertake.

The outer ring penetrated, the constricting lines drew in about the second ring, which was based upon the massive forts that German engineers had made more formidable with heavily mined approaches, antitank ditches, and outworks of steel and concrete machine gun emplacements. The fort in the 116th's sector was called Montbarey, and its glowering bulk dominated the ridge line along which we were advancing. The closing arc of fire about the city had brought the regiment's front down to battalion width, and the reduction of the fort fell to the lot of Tom Dallas's 1st Battalion, with the 2d and 3d in reserve.

On a gray, misty morning in mid-September, I went up to look over the operation to which we might be committed. The scene was grim, devastated landscape in which squatted the huge fort, like some felled monster, its hide frayed and worn by shell fire and bombs but not torn open.

Big Tom, as affable, demanding, and loud as he had been at the armory when we were mustered for the war nearly four years before, strode about directing engineers clearing a path through the minefield for a detachment of British Churchill flame-thrower tanks, with the thought that they could burn out the forts with the 1944 model of Greek fire. Tom invited me to stay, and I found it much more relaxing to watch, than to command, a battalion action. Tom was never one to make a muted effort; his demands for artillery and self-propelled gunfire to keep the Germans' heads down while the engineers worked could probably be heard at the regimental command post without benefit of telephone. He got the fire, but it did not entirely suppress the German riflemen, whose toll included a soldier standing within a few feet of Colonel Dwyer. Why the rifleman picked the small figure as a target rather than the broad shapes of the regimental and battalion commanders is in the endless realm of the unknowable. It could have been just poor marksmanship.

The fort and its outer works were blanketed by a heavy concentration of smoke laid down by chemical mortars, and the 121st combat engineers started probing and lifting mines and marking the cleared path with white tape. It was late afternoon before this was judged to be complete and four of the huge Churchills, towing their fuel trailers, began a roaring, clanking descent upon the fort. They moved in column; two left the cleared path and struck mines that the first tank had missed. The explosion blew one tank sideways and tore off a tread, blocking the path. Fortunately, the fuel trailer did not ignite. The tank commander brought his injured driver out of the minefield in his arms, followed by the rest of the crew. The lead tank continued alone. We saw it close with the fort and begin to shoot long, licking tongues of flame against the walls, a small dragon circling and searing a huge, downed prey before withdrawing for more engineer mine clearing.

Two more days of flaming and blasting were required to reduce Montbarey. Fort Keranroux, to our north, was taken by the 175th Regiment, and with the fall of these two strong points, the siege lines constricted again, drawing up against the last defensive ring, which was based on the old city wall. The wall lay largely in the 175th's sector, but with the ever-present possibility of boundary changes, the 2d Battalion was also alerted to prepare to assault it. For this contingency, the regiment's pioneers made ladders of timber so heavy and cumbersome that a squad was required to raise one. We did not have to try; the boundaries held, and the 116th's attack cleared the southern end of the wall and into the newer section of the city, called Recouverance. Not all opposition had faded, but it dwindled by the hour. Twenty-mm shells and machine gun bullets did not become more benign but were fewer and further between, and the crews more interested in surrender.

Recouverance was in a familiar state of ruin: houses gaping open, scorched by flames; streets blocked by rubble; and the whole smelling of cordite, dust, and charred wood. I had not given thought to what was happening to its citizens under this constant battering. As it turned out, most had been evacuated before the siege, but some remained. The second morning after entering the city, I was asked to come up to where some riflemen of F Company were halted in front of the ruins of a large church. With them was a middle-aged Breton of bearing and dignity. He asked me to accompany him into the church cellar where, by the irregular light of lanterns and candles, I saw men, women, and children with pale, tired faces. They had lived in that cellar for over a month. More in sadness than in celebration, he proffered a glass of wine and proposed a toast to the liberation of Brest and to their American Allies. There was in these people, who had endured four years of occupation, climaxed by the destruction of their city, an impressive dignity and quiet. In their presence, I felt in no way a liberator; it seemed more fitting to express regret than to accept appreciation. Unfortunately, my response to the toast fell between the two stools, and I wish I could have another chance at it; a second time, I would not try to smile reassuringly.

By nightfall, the 116th had reached its objective of the high ground overlooking the Bay of Brest. On our left, the 175th was into the old town through an unguarded tunnel under the wall. On our right, the 115th had hard fighting in reducing the strong positions ringing the submarine pens.

Then, in a single day, 18 September, it was all over. Simultaneously, it seemed, pockets of defenders concluded that it was idiotic to fight to the death to delay for a few more hours the capture of port facilities already destroyed. Surrender began everywhere; junior officers emerged from bunkers bearing white flags and, striving to save face, asked that surrender be to officers of the same grade or senior to their immediate commanders. Considerable rank had survived, and, in that war, a U.S. Army Corps did not carry around its equivalent. Under the circumstances, the defeated generals found military dignity a nebulous point to stand on, and so surrender took place to whatever rank happened to be handy: NCO or officer.

I had not seen POW hauls on the scale of the long lines of soldiers, sailors, marines, and airmen filing out from the underground shelters, carrying full packs and hand luggage: no Stalingrad or Bataan, this; no starving, disease-ravaged skeletons doomed to a fate as terrible as the one from which they had just escaped. Instead, the men Hitler had order to defend Brest to the death were well-fed, cleanshaven, and well-turned-out. They marched away smartly under sparse guard to finish the war in American prison camps, than which there were worse fates. I am sure that in the postwar years, the survivors of Stalingrad have looked down upon those of Brest as having played at war.

The 116th remained another day in Recouverance to guard the captured military installations, while the rest of the division was withdrawn to rest areas on nearby Le Conquet peninsula, which juts into the bay and the sea. The city was dead and silent except for the occasional rumble of a falling wall of masonry. The extra day there allowed an opportunity to look over the prize we had fought for. All exposed port facilities were in shambles, but the German wartime construction had held up well. The submarine pens, roofed with yards of reinforced concrete, were massive — on a scale that is particularly German. Underground warehouses, hospitals, command centers, and living quarters were equally enormous. The close-in machine gun and antiaircraft gun emplacements guarding all this were of tempered steel that our armor-piercing shells only dented at point-blank range. Had the defenders had a bent for an epic death stand, they were well-equipped.

Equally as impressive as the size of the installations were their stocks of supplies. Historically, the Stonewall Brigade had not seen such enemy bounty since the original command had shared in the happy acquisition of the Yankee depots at Manassas Junction eighty-two years before, on the way to the field of Second Manassas. The lean, ragged brigade of 1862 had marched with genuine hunger, and lack in all things material had whetted its appetite for enemy plenty. The 1944 brigade lacked for nothing material; there is, however, something of an elemental urge to acquire enemy property, and I doubt that any Stonewaller left Brest the next day without a memento.

A night on Le Conquet was required to realize that we were now removed by more than one hundred miles from battle, with which we had been in close embrace for all but a few days of the past three and a half months. With this realization, tension was shed like a dirty, sweat-stained uniform, and the clean garment of well-being was donned in the sun-warmed sea breezes of the Brittany coast. Unit journal entries starting 19 September are about hot meals, showers, and softball and football teams organized by Si Johnson, rather than repeating the previous litany of casualties, shelling, attack, and counterattack.

The journal also carries a deceivingly innocent entry about plans for furloughs for a proportion of D-day veterans being canceled. The close little world of an infantry battalion does not go long without a bone of contention to gnaw on; the projected furloughs supplied that need for the moment. They were to be to England, and immediate conflict arose over who was to get them. Knowing how much I depended upon the riflemen, I decided they were the most equal among equals. I also went so far as to suggest to Lieutenant Colonel Harold Cassel, the regimental executive officer, that I might be available. He suggested that I forget it. The question of the furloughs waxed hot for about a day and was ended by word that the plan was called off; we were to return to the war now smoldering on the borders of Germany. (Minor military maxim: The soldier who will not fight for a respite from the ranks usually will not fight when in them.)

There were four days of this relatively idyllic existence. I recall no schedule other than daily raising and lowering of the flag at retreat and reveille formations. These ceremonies were conducted with much less than parade-ground smartness but carried the particular authority of three months of battle. Swimming was authorized from beaches cleared of mines by the engineers, but the extensive rules to safeguard against accidental drowning made this more trouble than it was worth. I do not know if the object was to save soldiers for greater hazards, or because more paperwork is required for an accidental death by drowning than for one in battle. (Another minor military maxim: If it is not ironic, it is not war.)

Not noted in the unit journal is a dance that was organized by some of the battalion officers at a war-shabby resort hotel on the bay. The assembly did not outshine its surroundings. Although the French girls undoubtedly did their best, their frocks showed the effects of four years of occupation-enforced austerity, climaxed by the siege. The officers wore unpressed olive drab and combat boots with unshinably rough surfaces and composition soles with no glide qualities whatsoever. The only real adornment was youth, and I do not believe we were yet aware of how foreshortened this was. The dance was well-chaperoned by mothers who did not intend that their daughters be included in the ruin of the city. I readily signed a postal card composed by the hotel proprietor to General Charles De Gaulle, telling him how well his American Allies were being treated. This is my only communication to a head of state. General De Gaulle was involved with a chaotic array of crises and he may not have noted it. At least, he did not reply.

On 23 September, the brief interlude on Le Conquet ended. The battalion clambered again into trucks for a short haul to a railhead at Landerneau where we bivouacked overnight. The next morning, C-rations were issued, a depressing sign somewhat lightened by a USO (United Service Organizations) show and by a Red Cross doughnut-and-coffee wagon, which delayed for the moment the descent to ration-can level. Early that afternoon, we marched under full pack to the railyard, where stood a long train of freight cars — unchanged since World War I. The train had been made up for full companies, and, as we were at about two-thirds strength, it was possible to shade the ratio of forty men per car. The few extra feet of space was the only luxury available. Officers fared better in war-worn day coaches, compartmented as in the English trains. About midafternoon, the engine snorted and groaned and slowly set the cars in motion eastward. Behind was left yet another fresh war cemetery, and an abandoned solution to the problem of supplying the Allied armies.

There was no talk on the train as to whether Brest had been necessary or not. I doubt that anyone gave it thought. The 1st and 2d battalion officers shared a coach, and Tom Dallas had Bill Williams lead his favorite "limey" song about the rich getting the gravy and the poor getting the blame. The train rattled and clicked along and — a rite of passage appropriate to cargo and destination — emitted low, mournful whistle blasts on approaching towns and villages; these, also appropriately, appeared dead and deserted.

A soft, hazy September dusk drew on, and we delved into the too, too familiar depths of cold cans of minced ham and egg, followed by blocks of what seemed to be pressed sawdust faintly flavored by bitter chocolate — officially designated D-bars; there were, of course, expressed opinions as to whether the "D" represented durable, damnable, or even despicable.

The poor fare was compensated by excellent company, the fine product of the prodigal selection processes of the war. All were certified foot soldiers; credentials included a DSC, several Silver Stars, and more Bronze Stars. Purple Hearts and the Combat Infantry Badge were universal. In this little world, each man had a definite place and job, and to this extent each knew — if not always happily — who he was. All, too, had common objectives: first, survive; second, win the war and go home. For the moment, both seemed attainable. Although individual inner conflicts and anguish must have abounded, I believe that, on the whole, we were content with ourselves and, in varying degree, with one another.

Finally, talk and laughter stopped, and all in the swaying, rattling, black-out coach settled to rest in accustomed discomfort while the train inched across the curved surface of this small planet toward the large war momentarily marring its surface.

6

To the End

Years have passed since then and time mellows memories.

I Rode with Stonewall
Henry Kyd Douglas

For three days and into the fourth night, the troop train, sounding at intervals its lonely wail, clanked and clicked across France and into Belgium. In keeping with army movements in general, this was one of stops and starts. There were long halts on the war-worn rail system, and frequent slowdowns to cross hastily repaired bridges and culverts that had been blown by French Resistance saboteurs to hamper the German retreat. At Dreux, an accident ahead held us up for an entire afternoon. The boredom and discomfort of such travel, however, were borne with great patience, for we were returning to war. The halts allowed time to heat coffee and to trade with citizens for eggs, bread, and wine. Some months later, and not without reason, Americans were to be looked upon by many of the French as Allies overstaying their need, but, at the moment, liberation was still fresh and the liberators welcome.

As the train entered the heavily used main line supplying the front, we found the right of way paved with empty ration cans. At one halt, for lack of anything better to do, the two battalions policed these cans for the length of the train, piling them into huge cairns over head-high. Shaving and rudimentary washing were also possible during the stops, but, even so, after days of close living, the aroma around boxcars and coaches was probably pronounced.

149

Paris was passed on the third night, with hardly a pause in a vast, dark marshaling yard. I do not believe that anyone jumped train for the pleasures of Paris; in fact, I recall only one desertion during the journey, though there may have been more. The man I recall as having decided on an indefinite layover was returned by the military police just before the battalion reentered the battle. His company commander was troubled about what to do with him. We agreed that he had been a good enough soldier and would be of more use in the upcoming attack than in a stockade. The point that the battle line — land, sea, or air — is the place of honor is clouded by historical instances of convicted criminals being put into the fight at points where death was more predictable than at others — the avowed purpose being redemption. It is altogether puzzling: If death purifies the transgressing soldier, what more can it do for the nontransgressing? The biblically cited prodigal son and the lost sheep, somehow, do not seem to fit the case. In any event, at that time, we needed every man we could lay hands on. He was put back into the ranks, where I believe he was killed along with nondeserters.

The long journey ended on the dark night of 29 September, at Visé, Belgium, some twenty miles due west of the German border city of Aachen (the ancient Aix-la-Chapelle). Stiff from the lengthy confinement, and from the cold autumn-night air, the battalion detrained and clambered into trucks for a two-hour trip to the regimental assembly area near the town of Valkenburg. The motor train had made the trip from Brest by road and was already in the assembly area with kitchens set up and company areas laid out. There was every evidence that we had returned to the war: The truck convoy had been blacked out, as were houses along the way; far to the east was the pulsating glow of shell fire; in the dark, foxholes were dug to the depth of individual sensitivity. I believe the general emotional response to this was akin to that of workmen arriving on a job that they knew and had reason to dread. A cold, damp wind blew.

Morning emerged gray from a gunmetal dawn. Our bivouac was again among apple orchards, but different from those of Normandy. Here, the trees were tall, instead of low and gnarled, and they were heavy with large, sweet table fruit, rather than the small, sour, cider apples of Normandy. As might have been expected, an order came down that, for some forgotten health reason, the apples were not to be eaten; as might be expected, it received only outward compliance. (I recall no warning ever issued about the health hazards of combat.)

Winter gear — all wool and in the olive drab hue of that army — was issued this first day: long, heavy overcoats, sweaters, underwear, knit caps for wear under the cold steel helmets, and gloves. So clad and strapped about with ammunition belt and pack, a 140-pound soldier looked a robust 180. Unfortunately, he remained 140 pounds in strength and the more robust appearance was extra weight to carry. Not until the winter campaigns in Korea, six years later, was the army to develop a practical uniform for war in cold weather.

General Gerhardt came by that first afternoon and called for men from each company to gather around for a talk. Of this, I recall only that he asked if anyone knew a famous product of the region. This drew blank "soldier looks," so he said that we were in Limburg, home of the Limburger cheese, information that did not light up many faces; gastronomically, we were not that sophisticated. On testing Limburger, a soldier was bound to observe that the socks he had marched in for a week smelled better. Even so, it compared favorably with the cheese in the emergency ration, which tended toward plastic.

For four days, the regiment remained among the apple orchards in XIX Corps reserve. Long reconnaissance trips were made to areas where we might be committed in the assault on the Siegfried Line north of Aachen. The terrain, we found, was vastly different from Normandy and Brittany. Here, instead of small fields enclosed by hedgerows, there were long, open stretches without obstruction, bounded only by the horizon. As a variation, there were mining areas marked by rearing pit heads, huge pyramids of slag, and clusters of miners' homes. Overall, the scene was alien and foreboding under autumn skies. I actually missed the hedgerows and worried about attacking over ground that could be dominated for hundreds of yards by a section of machine guns.

Intelligence briefings, officer and NCO calls, firing on an improvised rifle range, and training in the division's battle drills filled the dwindling daylight hours and spilled over into dark. There were interludes of movies, and visits by the Red Cross doughnut wagon. A Special Services team appeared to take orders for Christmas presents to be delivered back home. The selection had wartime limitations; I ordered boxes of candy for my family that I do not believe were ever delivered.

Hope that the war might be over by Christmas — a traditionally projected time for ending wars — became dimmer. There were vague reports of the Allied airborne assault some eighty miles to the north that might have ended it had it succeeded in its object of turning the Rhine River barrier and opening a way into the Ruhr armament production area. Only after the war did I learn of the terrible losses of this attack on the Arnhem bridge over the Rhine, and along the narrow way to it.

During this period, before the mid-October battles began, I believe the 2d Battalion reached a peak of condition that it had not known since the eve of D-day: Ranks were reasonably full, and there was a strong cadre of battle-tested officers and NCOs throughout. Living was good, and men and equipment looked fit to the point of sleekness. The tearing away of this hard-won state of well-being was not to begin until 13 October, but once under way, it was fast and ruthless.

War began again earlier for other battalions of the division, which were committed during the first week of October in a number of bloody actions. In one of these, a rifle company and several tanks were lost attacking a town called Schierwaldenrath that had the fatal distinction of affording observation over an important stretch of highway. There were heavy losses in American and German lives in fighting over possession of this dismal view.

The war and the weather grew more sullen together. After 7 October, attacks were halted across the division's front, but for companies on the line in defensive positions this was little comfort, for it meant daily combat and reconnaissance patrols that had little to commend them over outright attack. For battalions in reserve, training was unremitting, with detailed demonstrations of how the general wanted things done, from battalion calisthenics conducted by commanders to firing exercises on offense and defense.

A platoon firing demonstration remains in mind by reason of three or four horses, probably made stray by the war, suddenly appearing at full gallop along a ridge directly in the line of machine gun and rifle fire. There was an involuntary murmur of dismay among the viewers, watching from a hillside behind the firing line, as the horses, in line astern and tails and manes flying — a beautiful and pathetic sight — appeared to gallop through the interlocking lines of tracer bullets. The firing halted momentarily and then resumed as the horses disappeared over the ridge, so far as I know unhurt. Anyone seeing them and caring for the great heart and beauty of the animals had to be glad that, after so many centuries, the horse was no longer a votive offering to war, not by reason of compassion, but by being too ineffective in modern combat to make a productive sacrifice.

The battalion journal records that on 6 October we moved to the vicinity of Kerkrade, in the Netherlands, closer still to the enemy's homeland. Near here, the next day, one of our communications jeeps exploded a land mine, and the four men in it were mangled to death. I considered our small crew of signal men as good as any in the army: They had kept the radios working within the technical limitations of the day, and the telephone lines always followed right on the heels of an advance; when shelled into pieces, the lines were repaired under fire without order or urging. At times, I thought it might be better if my superiors did not have such ready means of passing orders and pressure for progress, but balancing this was my frequent need for help. To lose such soldiers on a dreary dirt road to a casual exclamation of high explosive was a personal blow.

We were close enough to the front to see Allied fighter-bombers strafing, and in the evening a German plane came over, solo, dropping flares and then bombs that never hit in our sector.

Marches and countermarches continued as XIX Corps sought an opening to use its reserve battalions in a final drive to close the circle around Aachen. One of these sparring moves came 8 October. The battalion entrucked that night for a three-hour trip over unfamiliar roads that led, for the first time, into Germany, near the town of Alsdorf, where we arrived about 0200. It was two hours later before the companies were deployed in pitch dark in what I hoped was a reasonably sound defensive posture. We were in the area of a combat command of the 2d Armored Division, to which we were temporarily attached. With Si Johnson, I rode to its command post to announce our helpful presence and to try to find out what was expected of us — there being, always, residual fear that attachment to another outfit might mean assignment to its dirty work. The command post was in the cellar of a shell-blasted house that, even with its murky air, was preferable to the cold, windswept hole in the ground that was the 2d Battalion's command post. I reported to the duty officer and was surprised when he told me to wait while he awoke his general. I had not expected to be greeted and briefed at so high a level — generals were not so plentiful then; I recall seeing no more than four or five in the course of the war. This general, a slight, wiry man, undoubtedly a cavalryman, appeared a bit worn in the hard white pool of light from the buzzing gasoline lantern. Quietly enough, he traced the position of his tanks bulging into Germany. With an unreassuring smile, he observed that he did not expect to have us under his command long, but that if he did he would certainly use us; in the meantime, we were to stay where we were.

It was late dawn before we got back to the battalion, and late afternoon before the position had been realigned to conform to the high, barren swell of ground that daylight showed we occupied. After this, hot water was brought up from the company kitchens for shaving; I hope that it was accompanied by hot food, but memory and the battalion journal fail on this point. I would not be proud to have ordered a cleanshaven battalion in preference to one with warm food in its belly.

The 2d Armored general proved right about having a short lease on our services. The next day, 11 October, Colonel Dwyer came up to inform us that the regiment was now under the 30th Infantry Division to reinforce its drive southward to link up with the 1st Infantry Division, pushing north to isolate Aachen.

Over the past two weeks, I had come to appreciate the advantages of being part of a small reserve on a tautly stretched front. Once this reserve was committed, the corps commander would have little left to put into his battle, and so he was thrifty of it. To this, we owed our respite. But now, events were forcing all the chips onto the table; there was intense pressure from First Army to complete the capture of Aachen, and so the 1st and 2d Battalions of the 116th ceased marching up and down the corps sector and assembled at Bardenberg to attack and link up with the 1st Division on the main Aachen-Jülich highway supplying the German garrison. The Germans were reacting violently to every threat to this lifeline. Between us and the point of linkup was the sizable town of Würselen.

On the morning of 12 October, with the company commanders, I reconnoitered the attack position south of Bardenberg, a sector held by a battalion of the 30th Division's 119th Regiment. Beyond its thin line was a wide-open stretch, and then a built-up area of houses of North Würselen, which I was told was heavily defended. These defenses usually remained quiet until any forward move was made and then erupted small arms, tank, and artillery fire.

We returned to the battalion about noon and late that afternoon marched the four or five miles to the attack assembly area; in the distance, Allied fighter-bombers climbing, then diving and strafing. The attack was to go in at 0900 the next morning with the 1st and 2d Battalions abreast, supported by a company of light tanks of the 66th Armored Regiment. I conferred with the captain commanding the tanks, and we settled the standing question of who was to precede — tanks or infantry — by agreeing to go forward together. He was a quiet-talking soldier, and I believed (not necessarily by reason of his Southern accent) that he would carry his end of the attack.

The night was the usual restless one for me before a push, with much thought of what I might have done to prepare it better. Morning moved in, relentlessly cold and gray, and breakfast answered appetite in kind: cold and gray. Combat packs and weapons were shouldered, and we moved off in a column of companies to the line of departure — the last part of the approach march, made under the comforting overhead sighing of shells of the artillery preparation that raised a glow of explosions in North Würselen.

The tanks had also moved up under the noise of the artillery preparation and, right on the moment of 0900, riflemen and armor lurched forward. As it turned out, this was to be my last full day of battle, and on the macabre scale of war I think it registers as a good one. The tankers were aggressive and used all their firepower; the battalion had much experience and was as rested as an outfit can expect to be in war. Going in right behind the artillery preparation, infantry and armor made it across the open stretch and into the built-up area at the first bound. Here, the going became rougher. The journal records that, by 1400, there was heavy resistance from pillboxes, tanks, and artillery. My principal recollection is of calling Colonel Dwyer to tell him that we had advanced nearly a mile, had a number of prisoners, and were on our objective. Another mile and we would reach the highway and the linkup with the 1st Division.

This pride was short-lived. The penetration was long and narrow; the Germans may not have reacted to the opportunity this presented as rapidly as they would have earlier in the war, but, during the night, they began to build up along both of our long, open flanks.

The forward command post was in a cellar of a house about a block behind the front, and, taking stock of our situation on the map, I noted a parallel to Saint-Lô, barely three months before, when, after a long penetration, the battalion was cut off for days and barely survived. Such thoughts were insomnia-inducing. In the early morning hours, I tramped out into the garden behind the house, the dead vegetation crackling underfoot with early frost. There was utter darkness; the only evidence of the war was the strange undulating mutter that marks a battlefield at night: movements of armies supplying themselves for the next day's killings; the resting sounds of long lines of men; the sudden clash of patrols or nervous sentries; and questing salvos of artillery. That night, the conversation of combat was low and intermittent, but its sources curved around our flanks most ominously.

I considered calling Colonel Dwyer about my concern over pushing further into such surroundings. I had, however, seen enough of war to know that, at First Army and XIX Corps headquarters, the necessity to secure Aachen did not allow too much concern over the fate of a single infantry battalion. I can hope that no one up the chain of command uttered those generous words: "I don't care how many casualties it costs!"

Colonel Dwyer cared about casualties, and his map showed our situation as well as mine did. Too, the company commanders at the wire-thin cutting edge of the wedge had not troubled me with their fears, so I contained mine and roused the artillery liaison officer to call in fire around our position as a warning snarl of defiance, if nothing else. There was some argument over the field phone with the fire-control center, reluctant to expend shells on an unobserved target, but we invoked the authority of an outfit under the gun and exacted a few concentrations. Out in the garden again, I heard the shells sigh over and then saw the flashes as they crashed among houses a few blocks away. Under the circumstances, it seemed more a hesitant and nervous bark than a menacing growl.

So went the night away and lightened into cold, gray day. With it, we started again blasting forward on a front only about a city block wide, with the promise that help was coming up on either side. At the same time, German artillery and mortar fire began to mark our position with ear-blasting explosions and dirty-black clouds of burned cordite blossoming around. It was from one of these clouds that my leave from the battle emerged.

The time was not yet midmorning. I was standing with Si Johnson and the radio operator in the back doorway of the command post house. Mortar shells were dropping so thickly that the explosions seemed to merge. I do not recall any particular thoughts at the time, but, if true to form, I was wondering what could be done. If so, the answer came with a spectacular explosion at the far end of the winter-brown garden. Black smoke swirled upward, and I think I even heard the banshee wail of the piece of shell casing that hit me in the lower left leg with the impact of a hard-swung baseball bat. As much in surprise as anything, I went down. Si and the operator carried me to the cellar and laid me on my bedding roll. Raising up on an elbow — a characteristic posture, I had noted, of the wounded — I looked with some curiosity at my leg, which was numb enough to seem unrelated. The wound was narrow and perhaps two inches long; the skin around its edges ragged and dark but barely bleeding. Obviously this was grounds for claim to another cluster to my Great Good Luck Medal, already fairly crowded with clusters. Anywhere other than a leg or arm, it would probably have been final; as it was, I was now acceptably relieved from further responsibility for the war whose constant thudding noises penetrated to the cellar.

Not long afterward, Colonel Dwyer's bulk blocked out the lantern light. He growled that he was sorry I was hurt, and that I had done all right. Eccles Scott was there as executive officer and was told to take command. Had my emotions been less self-centered I would have felt sorry for anyone taking over in such a situation. Bloody fighting and heavy casualties were to attend further attempts to force a way through Würselen before the route was abandoned, and an attack mounted around the right of the town to achieve the linkup.

After the colonel left, Si Johnson went out and flagged down a tank that was en route to the rear for some tanker reason. Si carried me up the stairs and hoisted me onto the rear deck for a ride out of the war; the last I saw of a fine battalion staff was his good, square face looking concerned. If I felt any regret and sense of being a deserter, it was then. Later that same day, Si was hit in the leg by a shell fragment, with such damage as to require amputation.

The tank roared and lurched back over yesterday's route of attack, while I hung on to whatever cold metal projections offered a handhold. Shell bursts continued their dark flowering along the way, but none hit really near. At the edge of Bardenberg, I was shifted to a stretcher jeep and taken to the battalion aid station, where Doc Herter looked at my leg and wrote out a casualty tag. He changed the dressing and said cheerfully in his Puerto Rican accent not to worry, I would be back in no time. I told him not to expect me too soon. Some days before, he had said that he felt he could not stand more mangled bodies, but he did at Würselen, where the aid station was kept full, and even more during the November offensive. Knowing Herter's merit makes me think that I would not want a battalion surgeon who enjoyed treating wounds.

The jeep's other stretcher was loaded with a head-wound case, and we were jounced over the rough pavement to the division's medical clearing station. I was loaded directly into an ambulance, but the head-wound case was held for emergency treatment. The enclosed ambulance had brackets for stretchers in tiers on either side. All I recall of the ride back to the field hospital was that, when the doors were closed, it was dark inside, that the man in the stretcher above me became sick, and that another one, across the narrow space between us, moaned constantly.

Treatment was more detailed at the field hospital. I was put in a long ward tent, and again memory is hazy except that there were rather frequent injections. I also recall that from the nurses' station, curtained off by canvas, came sounds of a nurse enjoying hysterics in an accent that could only have been nurtured near the New York subway. Her high-pitched plaint was about something crawling in her ear. Another nurse was trying to calm her, but my diagnosis, based on extensive experience, was that the patient did not intend to respond to treatment on the European side of the Atlantic; a therapeutic slap might have done wonders, rendered only, of course, by a peer in gender and rank.

Another tent nearby was filled with wounded POWs, who were singing a lengthy program in chorus. The singing was hearty and tuneful, though I could not tell if the songs were in praise or lament of Germanic life, love, or war. Altogether, hospital quiet did not prevail, but, luxuriating in freedom from responsibility, opportunity for rest, and probably under the influence of a sedative, I was untroubled and slept.

Details of my passage along the medical pipeline, except for some scenes, are hazy. I recall an overnight trip on a comfortable hospital train to Paris; a team of medical corpsmen came through administering penicillin with what seemed unusually dull needles. Ambulances made the transfer from train to a large, civilian hospital. Corpsmen unloading us at the hospital were insistent with questions about war souvenirs for sale; one, lifting my stretcher, was complaining loudly to his partner about being denied a pass into the city. I said I would be glad to try to get him a pass to Würselen, but I do not believe the point registered.

The hospital must have been one of the plush ones of Paris, for it showed much tile, marble, and highly polished dark wood. Here, the metal was removed from my leg. The part I had dreaded was being put to sleep by ether, whose choking fumes I remembered from a childhood operation. The easy oblivion induced by sodium pentothal, of which I had not heard, was such a relief that it displaces memory of discomfort from the long slice in my leg, which was for the time left open. I awoke in a room of such opulence that, in other times, it must have been occupied privately by the wealthy ill. Now, it was crowded with beds in one of which was Ed Gearing, an aggressive young lieutenant of the 116th who had won a DSC on the beach and had picked up several Purple Hearts and other worthwhile ribbons since. We talked about his hometown of Woodstock, Virginia, where I had once published a weekly newspaper. Otherwise, I read and slept and wrote home about being out of the battle and not seriously hurt. The letter arrived before the War Department telegram used to announce casualties, which was fortunate, for it was a time when families dreaded receiving telegrams.

Wreckage from the Aachen front arrived every day. I was nourishing my immobility, and not getting about, but some of the walking wounded from the battalion came by with bloody tales of Würselen. They said the

159

battalion had been reduced to a new low in strength and recited a sad list of deaths. There were also personal matters. One soldier said quite seriously that he was due to return to duty and that his tendency to wet his bedroll would make living intolerable in the cold weather that was coming on. He asked that I help him get a transfer to the South Pacific, where his problem would not be so uncomfortable. He finally convinced me that he was not joking, but I am sure that he was convinced that nothing other than meanness kept me from arguing his perfectly logical case before a medical board.

The chore of censoring letters followed right into the hospital. Out of a batch to which I was giving perfunctory glances and initialing, one from a hospital corpsman caught my attention. This is not an exact quote, but it is the sense of his letter home from Paris, a hundred miles behind the front: "Wait! I hear rifle shots! I'll have to go see about it." Later — "Well! I took care of that German, now I can continue. . . ." I reread this several times in wonder and then initialed and sent it on: Cleaning wards and carrying bedpans is an essential job, and men performing it should have some leeway in telling their part in the great world war.

After a week in Paris, the pressure of incoming casualties from the heavy fighting along Germany's borders pushed my mid-October class of wounded further back along the medical pipeline. I became part of another hospital train, shipped off to a tent hospital in Normandy, a dreary place of brown canvas, brown landscape, and unrelieved gray skies. Here, I made tentative efforts to walk and found my leg beset by jabbing needles, and the foot flopping out of control. For the first time, it occurred to me that this wound might not have its originally estimated million-dollar value. The surgeon said that it might respond to therapy, but he believed there should be another operation, and that best done back in England.

I opted for his recommendations and so was bundled up, tagged, supplied with multicopy orders, and loaded at night on a British hospital ship at Cherbourg for a morning run across the Channel. It was now November. The Channel was rough with wind and rain and did nothing to improve the opinion I had formed of it on 6 June. The British hospital breakfast ran to porridge, tea, and bread — no improvement on the fried

Spam, powdered eggs, canned fruit, and coffee that dominated our American hospital menus.

England looked gray, misty, and good — next best to home. Another train ride took me to a large hospital in the Midlands, where further repair was done on the leg. Within a week, I was getting about with a cane and considering how to tread the fine line between well enough to obtain leave but not fit to go back to war. Hospitals, which had seemed such a haven, were beginning to pall, their routine a burden, and I longed for some civilian life.

Other than the assurance that I would not have to limp through the remainder of life, about all I remember of that stay was a wheelchair race between two single-leg amputees. Elaborate measures were taken by the race's sponsors to clear a gangway, around the rules, and the two racers went careening down the narrow concrete way to the cheers of the detachment of patients and little regard for the damage they might do themselves. The glee, I believe, was mostly for the triumph over authority. The young racers finished safely, flushed and laughing; the midnight of the soul that I think must sooner or later strike for every cripple had not yet struck for them.

During my month in hospital, the 2d Battalion had remained in the Würselen salient under artillery battering and counterattack, until it was worn down beyond use and withdrawn. After rest and refit, it was committed with the Stonewall Brigade in the November offensive that carried to the west bank of the Roer River. The few veterans who survived both Normandy and the November–December fighting for Koslar and Jülich told me that the latter was worse because of the freezing rain and fanatical Germans fighting on home ground. The all-pervasive mud, which they had to embrace to survive, fouled weapons as thoroughly as sand and salt water had on Omaha Beach; trench foot, influenza, and pneumonia apparently fed on both sides impartially.

In early December, Hitler completed the assembly of some thirty-two to thirty-six infantry and panzer divisions, and two thousand guns, for a final offensive that was to break upon four American divisions facing the Ardennes Forest in the dark of the winter morning on 16 December. That the beleaguered enemy could secretly concentrate such a massive bolt sent shock waves throughout the Allied world, and, against all reason, raised the specter of a lost war.

While all this went on, I was being propelled toward the exit of the hospital system. An analogy to passage through the birth canal would be strained if followed all the way, but it is valid to a degree. There were no audible wails from those leaving the warmth and safety of good mother hospital's womb for the cold, deadly world of war on the Rhineland Plain, but, undoubtedly, there were inaudible groans. In my case, a rather long interval between the system's final muscular contractions expelling me was spent in a convalescent hospital located not so far from Stratford- on-Avon. We were housed in a collection of igloo-shaped, corrugated-iron Nissen huts; the patients were for the most part infantry lieutenants and captains. Each was periodically evaluated to determine his state of recovery and fitness for further war. Like class standing in service schools, results of these physical evaluations were of avid interest to us all, with the difference that few sought to be at the departing top of the class.

My arrival at this hospital was just before the Germans launched the Ardennes offensive. First reports were vague and disarming as to its extent and power. I was much more occupied with nearly two months of accumulated mail that had caught up with me than with sketchy news stories about heavy fighting on the First Army front. A long string of victories stretching back to North Africa had conditioned us to expect more of the same, to the point where there could be no more German retreat and the war would end. Without giving it more thought than could be expected of a battalion officer, I shared in the general conviction that the enemy was close to complete disintegration, a belief that powerfully aided his purpose. Over the next six weeks, concern waxed as the tide of the offensive reached its height and then waned as it spent itself and receded. The only direct effect upon the hospital was to speed up the fitness evaluations.

While just about every division in the European Theater of Operations was represented among the patients, all had been wounded in October or before and knew no more about the battle than could be learned from confusing newspaper accounts. Primarily, we were interested in whether our friends were caught up in it; each believing firmly, on the basis of past experience, that his division was bearing the brunt. We were certainly nothing if not parochial: I was bored by war stories of other outfits, and at the same time surprised that no one was aware of the 29th's accomplishments, especially those of its 116th Regiment.

Not until rejoining the war, by then across the Rhine, did I learn that the 29th had stayed in the positions it had won in November along the Roer River opposite Jülich, and suffered primarily from the weather while the Battle of the Bulge raged to the south. Postwar revelations are that the German General Staff strongly favored launching the offensive along the Roer rather than through the Ardennes. The outcome would probably have been the same, but the fate of the 29th, directly in its path, would have been bloody.

While the Ardennes ordeal followed its bitter course, I, with some feeling of guilt, continued the pleasant life of convalescence. There were daily therapy sessions in the whirlpool tub, and I rolled marbles around with my foot. NCOs conducted long sessions of calisthenics and took us on what were called road marches but were largely walks with more straggling than formation. Convalescing officers proved no more amiable to discipline than were officer students at Fort Benning. I was more tolerant in 1944, for these young officers had paid their way, and, undoubtedly, more was to be asked of them. My ward contained some twenty to thirty lieutenants and captains who possessed a notable array of freshly healed physical scars, and probably a number of unhealed emotional ones.

Evenings were free, and the neighboring town's pubs disgorged some loud and unsteady patients at closing time. For those who stayed in hospital, there were movies and discussion groups. At one of these, a heavyset English woman expounded upon the virtues of communist Russia. She was not a very attractive or persuasive speaker and, from the start, raised the hackles of an audience that might not have had much capital at the time but intended to acquire some once the war was over. The exchange between speaker and audience became heated on the instant, and the session ended abruptly.

I had not failed to let everyone I knew in England that I was back under honorable circumstances and so spent leaves visiting in Surrey and in London. Footlockers containing our better-class uniforms had been taken up and stored before D-day, so I had only a field uniform that I thought to dignify with the Combat Infantry Badge and by using a cane. This did not prove sufficient, and I was turned away from the officers mess in London. As my social life was showing promise, I shopped among the Bond Street tailoring houses until I found a fit in an Eisenhower jacket and pink trousers that had been made for an Air Corps officer who had run out of either life or money and had never claimed them.

Back at the hospital for Christmas, I found the NCO staff disturbed over a comb-out of the logistical system for replacements to make up the losses in the Ardennes. They were conscientious and hard-working at their difficult job of hastening the recovery of patients who were in no particular hurry to recover and risk more, and possibly worse, injuries, but, knowing how badly medical corpsmen were needed in the infantry, I could not sympathize with their distress too much. With a little pressure, the officer patients could have very well managed their own exercise sessions and road marches. A number of infantry battalions could have been assembled from the administrative and logistical people in England, alone, with nothing more damaging to the war effort than perhaps a slowdown in such functions as distribution of sports equipment.

The somber news from the Ardennes was a heavy shroud over Christmas. Attendance at church services was larger than usual; there was a holiday dinner, but little joy. Christmas Day started overcast, and in the afternoon the most opaque fog I experienced in England cut visibility completely and canceled invitations to Christmas tea from English families in the area.

Early in January, a fellow patient and I were ordered to temporary duty in Paris for job interviews at the Supreme Headquarters. This seemed a pleasant boondoggle, and a way out of hospital routine, so, bearing travel orders that included authorization for $1.25 a day for food, we went to London to await a flight to Paris. We languished in the chill, gray city for about a week before our low priority got us on a plane from Heathrow Airport to Paris, the passengers sitting on metal benches down either side, and cargo stowed in the center. Orly Airport, where we landed, was largely a shambles. We traveled into the city in an open jeep, arriving at the Place de la Concorde in the late afternoon of a clear winter day, and had an unobstructed first view of the length of the Champs Elysées up to its crowning glory, the Arc de Triomphe. War had removed all traffic other than a few stray military vehicles, and the way stood forth in full, uncluttered magnificence. The Champs soon returned to a crowded passage of people and cars, but I never see it without remembering it unmarred.

At a billeting office, our orders were given careful scrutiny, for Paris was filling with soldiers with concocted reasons for stopping there while the war raged to the east. The black market — especially in cigarettes, gasoline, and medical supplies — that started on the first day of the city's liberation was reaching such proportions as to deprive the front; a notorious case involving an entire railway-operating battalion engaged in wholesale looting and sale of supplies was coming to light. The desertion rate was equally scandalous, with the equivalent of a division of fugitives estimated to be in the Paris area alone. I felt equally execution-minded toward black marketers and deserters.

We were assigned billets in a second- or third-class hotel in Pigalle, and that evening toured the district's night life, which was operating at full throttle.

The next day, we were interviewed for personnel jobs that sounded so deadly dull that I made an unnecessarily bombastic declaration about considering myself still a member of the Stonewall Brigade and not wanting a change. Holman was equally unenthusiastic, and I believe we were written off as types arrogant over having been shot at. We were ordered back to England and the hospital.

With February, the Germans' winter offensive collapsed, and consciences were eased over languishing in the relatively posh surroundings of convalescence. At each medical evaluation, the doctor found my mobility improved; his lenient nature may have stretched my stay longer than necessary. I was busily caught up in hospital routine and in making the notes on the war that supply much of the memory for this book, so I did not dispute his professional judgment.

Finally, in early spring, I was declared fit for field service and ordered back to the 29th Division, which had by then passed the Roer River and also the Rhine. In a group of convalesced officers, I again made the trip to London and by plane to Orly. Here, we loaded onto trucks and headed eastward without so much as a pause in overcrowded, off-limits Paris.

The way back through the replacement pipeline was slow and tedious even though I had orders directly to the 29th. For those who were waiting to be allocated to where the need was greatest, the process was even more wearing. The end of the war now loomed unmistakably through the news headlines, and whatever urgency the replacement system had felt during the winter offensive had noticeably relaxed. Too, there seemed a desire in many, who had been content in France until now, to get into Germany for the kill. This crowded the roads with convoys of outfits ranging from optical supplies to shoe repair.

Our replacement convoy staged through depots that were variously housed in tents and in old French barracks. On an early spring day during the first week of April, I crossed again into Germany, now bearing the marks of thorough defeat. The principal building of every village through which the trucks rolled bore the sign of a military government detachment; the few civilians plodding about were mostly elderly and did not look up as we went by.

Near Wessel, we crossed the great Rhine, muddy and fast-flowing, over a slightly undulating pontoon bridge, and entered the rear area of the Ninth Army, then advancing toward the Elbe River some two hundred miles beyond. There was a final stop at a corps replacement depot, where I was put in charge of a hundred or so soldiers assigned to the 29th. A few were veterans returning from hospital, but most were new men fresh (though that is hardly an accurate word after their trip through the replacement pipeline) from the States. Included were a few black soldiers, as tentative moves were being made toward integrating the army — a process that a few more weeks of critical developments in the Ardennes would have hastened.

It was not a very sharp-looking crew, and I had some qualms over appearing at their head in the shaped-up territory of the 29th. Should we by chance encounter General Gerhardt, my return would be less than triumphant. About all I could do about this was to see that chin straps were buckled, that baggy pantlegs were bloused over boot tops, and that the trucks kept proper interval; that and to deliver my charges to the division's training center as soon as possible.

We rolled along through shattered villages and past engineer, ordnance, and quartermaster depots. With the first sight of the division's blue and gray shoulder patch came a curious feeling; the past four months were the longest I had been away from its intense life for four war-crowded years, and events of those past ten months made it seem even longer. Then I began to note changes, both marked and subtle, from the division I had left. The most marked was that of soldiers with the helmet strap buckled around the back rather than on the point of the chin. This was so surprising that it was the first thing I inquired about on arrival at the divisional command post. I was told that the general had relaxed his set-in-cement rule and that now the strap could be worn any way except dangling. A more subtle change was in the atmosphere: All was still ordered and businesslike, but somehow easier. I lingered there only long enough to pick up assignment orders to the 116th, then on the march toward the Elbe River.

Riding in a courier jeep and overtaking the rear of the regimental supply train, there was a feeling of entering the neighborhood of one's youth after long years away. There were the familiar sights and sounds of the regimental command post just going into bivouac, and familiar faces in new positions: Colonel Bingham was regimental commander; three of my OCS classmates held the principal staff jobs. There was the comfortable feeling of being back in surroundings I knew so well. The cushy war now, they told me, was hardly to be mentioned in the same breath with the one waged the past winter. Everything, including the weather, had broken bad after Würselen. Battle names, unfamiliar to me, such as Siersdorf, Engelsdorf, Koslar, Hasenfeld Gut, the Sportplatz, and Jülich, were spoken of as lingering nightmares. Losses of the 116th had totaled the equivalent of a full-strength battalion. A casualty that hit me deeply was that of Berthier Hawks, who was killed leading his rifle company. I had found him to be of exceptional character and thought he would go far.

Lieutenant Colonel Gene Meeks was now commanding the 2d Battalion, and I was assigned as his executive. He was a veteran of the regiment and a D-day battalion commander. I was pleased to finish out the war with the old outfit under his command. My return was received casually enough; after nine months of constant turnover, there was little notice of coming and going; some men had been wounded, evacuated, and returned twice and three times. The corps personnel officer who had stirred my ire at Vire by speaking of the battalion as a machine with replaceable parts was right. There were a few veterans who had come all the way, and their faces and movements showed it. Apologetically, they had to ask when it was that I had left; one thought I had been killed.

The German defenses were everywhere broken through from the east and from the west. I then learned that the Elbe River was designated for the political and military junction of the Allied and Soviet armies. A relaxed air extended to the front. Losses for the past month had been low, and, with heavy traffic returning from hospital, the ranks were full. This, combined with certainty of victory, the promise of spring, and the satisfaction of campaigning in the enemy's country and having access to his possessions, gave a pleasant aspect to the war. The few jeeps and weapons carriers allotted an infantry battalion became so laden with "trophies" that their weapons cargo was smothered.

Our march northeastward toward the Elbe River was through countryside, hamlets, and small towns. Houses invariably had bed sheets hung from windows as rumor spread among inhabitants that this sign of surrender would forestall destruction of their property. I do not think there was as much thought of destruction as there was of acquisition. German inhabitants were sparse and were largely the old and the very young. In one house was a bed-ridden elderly woman, and a note in rough English asking that she not be harmed as she was a good person and had always thought highly of Americans. We were surprised that we should be considered a menace to flee, and that we had to be importuned not to harm an invalid.

A greater hazard to German health and possessions were the thousands of slave laborers who were released from bondage to swarm over the countryside. They were from every nation that had been occupied by the German armies; human attributes had been brutalized, worked, and starved out of them. They had kept Germany's war machinery going and now felt license to wreck that machinery and its directors. They were humanity reduced to very nearly its lowest level, though they were responsive to being herded and directed. They were part of the dregs of the bitter tea that Germany had brewed for itself in five years of war. Collecting these people, euphemistically tagged "displaced persons," and caring for them became a major job during the advance.

They had little idea of what had happened and even less of why it had happened. Language differences and ancient national animosities seemed to run as deeply between them as against their masters. So, they had to be separated by nationality into camps that immediately took on the appearance of the worst city stews: cooking, toilet, and sleeping conducted side by side. With us, they were docile and friendly but totally uncomprehending of instructions on sanitation. At that time, DDT was considered a boon, not a hazard, to mankind, and it was blown into their thickly populated hair and clothing while they laughed in complete trust that whatever strange things these Americans did was all right.

The march also met parties of Allied POWs who had escaped or been abandoned by their captors. These lean, ragged men had fared better than the slave laborers, but they had the wary, hard look of captivity, which for some had been as long as four years. There were loaded onto trucks and continued on their way with no outward signs of rejoicing.

So, the ugliness and chaos that the war had engendered unfolded as we trudged deeper into Germany: a diorama of death, destruction, and depravity — everything but the ultimate obscenity of the extermination camps, which were not encountered in our particular zone.

The unit journal records that the march to the Elbe took four days, 20–24 April. I recall two of them as miserably wet and cold. The general's rule that the division live outdoors, no matter what the weather, had also been relaxed, so the nights were spent in the best houses, stoking the big porcelain heating stoves and sleeping in beds under bulky feather bolsters that tended to slide off onto the floor. The opportunities of campaigning in enemy country were quickly discovered. We had not lived so well in the past four years.

Such prosperity had its particular military price. Collecting booty became a principal occupation, overloading trailers and packs. To get to mortars and machine guns required digging down through layers of "souvenirs." I saw an angry first sergeant going down his company's vehicle column throwing the collections of junk piled on them into the ditch. As soon as he disappeared, it was piled back on. A report got around that

169

valuables were buried in yards, so mine detectors were brought out in a more enthusiastic search than had ever been made for mines.

All this wrought some not-so-subtle changes. From a hard, healthy preoccupation with self-preservation and victory, the battalion became interested in easy living and possessions. Drinking was more of a problem as wine supplies were found. Nonetheless, old patterns of discipline and performance did not disappear overnight. The march went on through villages that had unmanned trenches and antitank barricades. Death and injury still skulked along the way, mostly in the form of mines, one of which blew a tank destroyer apart; another killed the division's engineer officer.

Just before reaching the Elbe, the 116th encountered a German battle group fresh from occupation duty in Norway, but this, our last pitched battle of the war, was hardly started before it was over. All three of our battalions were put in against the woods where the battle group was making its stand. There were the familiar ripping sounds of high-cyclic fire from automatic weapons, which I had not heard since the previous October, and the crash of artillery. White flags appeared, and it was all over.

Another short march, and we closed along the banks of the Elbe, whose waters, like those of the Rhine, are wide, muddy, and rushing. This was a demarcation line, along which the Iron Curtain of communism was soon to descend. On that 24 April 1945, the far shore showed only the misty green curtain of early spring. We had, I believe, some instinctive wariness of the Red Army's approach, but also an awareness that without the terrible, costly war it had waged, we would still be fighting and dying. The assurance of German POWs that we would soon be fighting this ally was taken as the wishful thinking of the defeated.

For ten days, the battalion manned a long sector of the 29th's forty miles of the river line. Outposts were small and widely spaced, and there was a feeling that danger was past. It is another period foreshortened in memory; one of climax and anticlimax, war and peace, relief from the uncertainty of surviving the next hour, and a new uncertainty of the future. There was, however, a generally fixed intent to seek that future as soon as possible, out of uniform, and in the United States.

Death did not allow the last sands of the war to run out unused. On a moonless spring night, a German patrol crossed the river and shot up an outpost, killing a young soldier, the battalion's last death of the war. I suspect that the entire outpost had been confidently asleep. Each night, a few artillery shells from across the Elbe would crash in — enough to encourage me to take up sleeping quarters in the cellar of the large, brick command post house. The distinction of being the last casualty was widely unsought. The weather was generally fair the field of either side.

By day, row boats put out from the far side of the river, flying white rags and loaded with men, women, and children electing American mercies over Russian. Not only was our reputation for charitable treatment better, but we had far less reason for vengeance. In the 175th's sector, an entire German V-2 Rocket Division, over ten thousand men, surrendered with their equipment and were ferried across into captivity. That few drownings occurred was considered by both sides evidence of a well-conducted operation.

On 2 May, a patrol of the 175th crossed the Elbe and made contact with a Russian cavalry division. Pro forma celebrations followed with exchanges of vodka, whiskey, and embraces. The Russians were reported to be tough and formidable-looking. Their loot was carried in huge, horse-drawn German wagons. None appeared opposite our sector, and German refugee crossings continued more frantically.

Death hit high places during these spring weeks. On 12 April, word was flashed of President Roosevelt's passing at Warm Springs, and of a man named Truman being sworn in as president and commander in chief. The successive Roosevelt administrations had covered all my adult life, and it was hard to think of anyone else in charge. Then, while we were on the Elbe, Hitler did himself in among the ruins of Berlin. His gruesome end was noted as another step toward the now foregone conclusion to the war, and incidentally as serving the ends of justice. My own war world was too confined and far-removed from such positions for there to be an agonized reaction to the one, or elation over the other.

On 3 May, the 29th was ordered from the Elbe line to occupy an enclave around the North Sea cities of Bremen and Bremerhaven, designated as ports for supplying the U.S. forces. The move was by truck convoy, our last of the war. Having traveled this way for the past five years, it was considered routine, preferable to marching, though just as dusty in dry weather, and as cold and wet in rain. The division rule was that materiél, but not men, rode under cover.

For this last move of the wartime battalion, we rode in the elephantine two-and-a-half–ton trucks along a well-paved *Autobahn*, passing German POWs marching down the median strip carrying full packs and hand luggage. The weather was generally fair; the fields on either side, keeping their own springtime march schedule, were advancing shades of green. We were young and — figuratively — victors on horseback, looking down upon trudging captives, so we must have been content with our lot. (Not to involve God in such folly, I shall say that there but for the inscrutable workings of chance, and bad judgment of their Nazi leaders, went we along the median strip.)

The halt for the night was in a small town near Münster, where the division was assembling to move into the occupation enclave. As victors, we requisitioned the best houses for billets, and here, early the next morning, a glimpse of future violence flashed across the sky, shocking in noise and velocity. Unrecognized, for we had not heard of such a thing, what we saw was a jet fighter plane of the Luftwaffe on what could have been its last sortie of the war, screaming over just above the rooftops, appearing and disappearing so fast that the only reaction was apprehension. It was some time before I learned that this was the last of that dread triumvirate — guided missile, atomic-nuclear weapons systems, and jet plane — to appear in rudimentary form during the last year of the war. Successive generations of this trio have since dominated world fears and give the war's end a cast as ominous as its start.

We were still in the assembly area on 5 May, when complete German surrender was announced and Victory in Europe proclaimed. The 2d Battalion's reaction was not boisterous: Truck horns were sounded, a few rifle shots were fired in the air, and there was tapping of German wine stocks. In general, though, the foot soldier's reaction was subdued and, it seems to me, in keeping with the mood in which he had fought the war: conviction, determination, unstinted effort, no little courage and sacrifice — and little exultation. The raucous celebrations in Allied cities represented, I think, opportunity as much as true jubilation.

★ To the End ★

So, World War II in Europe shuddered to an end — a term used advisedly, for obviously such a cataclysm can have no absolute points of start and stop: Before the first shots and after the last stretch endless tangles of cause and effect, chance and mischance. And just as the war cannot be made into a tidy narrative package with no dangling ends, neither can be this remembrance of it. A prologue and now an epilogue pick up some strands leading into it, and some straggling out around its edges after its declared close.

For an infinitesimal moment the guns were silent. Sadly enough human conflict that triggers them never missed a step in its unending march. It was immediately apparent that the guns would speak again, and again.

Epilogue

Regarding war memoirs in general: I have noted that those of senior leaders tend toward supporting their decisions — and I do not say this critically, for their wars are things of unimaginable responsibility and of momentous choices that historians will long examine; they should present their briefs. On the other hand, long, backward looks at war from the lower levels seem to me to tend to brooding: over how chance sorted life and death, and fear constantly challenged pride and honor, and how after so great an effort and cost, nothing was basically changed. And, finally, what there was that one would want to remember at all. Obviously, however, there is an innate human need to remember wars, and so, as of VE-day, ends this conglomerate of things remembered as a foot soldier in the great 1939–1945 war: things heard, seen, felt, smelled, tasted, relished, regretted; things known, and surely some so keenly imagined as to seem known. These last I have truly sought to label so — this, and to avoid as far as possible the temptation of the "if only" school of war writing deploring, now that most answers are in, what was done when all answers were obscure, and few things were as they appeared.

VE-day is, on the whole, a logical stopping point. The articles of surrender signed in the schoolhouse in Reims certified the violent death of a regime that, having had terror and violence as policy, had no other possible end. Their mission achieved, the armies, navies, and air forces gradually retired from center stage to become, again, menacing spearcarriers in the background — clashing weapons and muttering on cue from the political players who again came forward. The juxtapositioning of enemies and allies resumed, and all continued lurching on into the unknown, howling from largely self-inflicted hurts, flailing wildly about when interests collided, and, perversely, achieving moments of dignity, courage, and even charity. The course of history that was deflected at such great cost away from one set of political and social wrongs took bearing and set course for others, equally ominous. Obviously, there is no getting to Utopia from here.

Peace declared, men of the 2d Battalion joined in the unseemly armywide scramble to get home and out of uniform. Veterans departed first, their places filled by later arrivals in the theater who had no less a homing urge. I spoke to one such group, stressing their good fortune on assignment to the illustrious 29th, but their only expressed interest was in when the division was to be demobilized. The individual order of going was based upon points for such as length of combat service and for wounds, bringing forth a seriously submitted claim on the basis of scratches from German barbed wire. By the time I left in October, few remained who had seen service back as far as Würselen.

For the Western Allies, the elation of standing upon the broken, groaning body of the defeated did not long remain unmixed. Soon, there was an urgent need to rejuvenate this enemy as an ally in the burgeoning clash with the Soviet Union. Other healing agents were at work: Those among whom we took up station as conquerors accepted their lot without excessive groveling or complaint. While we feasted on the rich fare of victors, they existed on the scraps salvaged from total defeat — a disparity that could not continue among peoples of similar cultures, energies, and abilities. Compassion for the vanquished developed along with self-interest (the two being mutually supporting), though evidence was still fresh and bloody that the majority of Germans had followed compassionless leaders with their lives and fortunes in a national cult as dark, ugly, and destructive as any in history. An early effort by the Allied command to maintain the German as mortal enemy by forbidding fraternization was quickly made nonsense by the transcending attraction between young men and women, and by the innocent appeal of children.

The light of reconciliation and reconstruction was hardly a dim glow on the horizon during my last days with the Stonewall Brigade along the shores of the North Sea. These were rare, luminous autumn days, sunlight glinting

176

off the dark water, the flat coastal fields and lines of trees brushed brown, red, and yellow. The air was heady and mild, though an occasional wind had the bite of a dour North Sea winter coming on. Driving through this bright glory on a round of goodbyes to the few old friends remaining in the regiment, I was aware that a strongly woven pattern of people, habits, and purposes, of which I was a part, was coming unraveled and would not be rewoven; it was the autumn of a year and of a personal era.

Departing the Stonewall Brigade was as unmarked as joining it had been. By way of incidental symbolism, however, the weather had changed overnight to gray; sharp slants of rain soaked the bright landscape, running its colors to darker hues. Battalion headquarters was in a handsome brick building that had been built with American contributions after the 1914–1918 war as a sanitarium for German children suffering from blockade-induced malnutrition. After breakfast there, I said goodbye to Colonel Meeks and the staff, loaded bag and baggage onto a jeep and, with a driver, rattled away through the imposing entrance to the grounds, headed for Paris and a short course at the Sorbonne, sponsored by the French government for Allied soldiers. The course was on French history and culture (with no exams); I rationalized it as a logical way to taper off from the war.

Perhaps it was around this leave-taking that the past four years began to take on the aspects of a lasting, long, and often-troubled dream — the sort one can have when enough awake to be aware of dreaming but curiously reluctant to end it. On leaving, there was, too, a surprising sense of regret for a regimented life ended, where I had thought there would be anticipation of an unregimented life resumed. The war years had left a mark of which I had not been aware; there would be no erasing it.

The route to Paris lay through the port of Bremerhaven, and then through Bremen, whose cathedral, somehow intact after years of saturation bombing, loomed above the ruins. All the German cities I had seen were in this ravaged state, and I could not imagine them as ever becoming any other way. Nor could I see brighter prospects for the gray towns of Belgium and northern France, dark and deserted-looking in the constant rain, through which we drove. The only traffic encountered was an occasional military vehicle.

★ Epilogue ★

The economic "miracle" that was to develop in Western Europe — notably in West Germany — over the postwar years could not be imagined by anyone traveling through that wrecked and hungry continent in the autumn of 1945. I had grown up in Tennessee on the prideful story of the South's reconstruction after Appomatox, but I could see no such potential in the dreary wastage of war unfolding before me. Apparently, firsthand experience of at least one war and its aftermath is necessary to understand what the efforts of millions of productive people can accomplish under the imperative of necessity and opportunity of freedom — and, in this instance, with the aid of the United States.

With the new year of 1945, the 29th came home. By then, it bore little resemblance to the hard-muscled infantry division of even six months before; now, it was largely an administrative headquarters for the return of homesick soldiers from all over the European Theater. After serving this mundane purpose, the division was dismissed from federal service at Camp Kilmer, New Jersey, just shy of five years after it had been mustered for war with purpose and panoply. The stand-down was accomplished by a brief War Department order, replete with abbreviations; the division history recounts that no bands played; certainly, no crowds cheered. The division reverted to its prewar National Guard status, with units in Maryland and Virginia. In 1968, in keeping with the antimilitary mood of the nation, it was retired to the inactive list; the component units remained on state duty.

The United States' attitude toward its military is nothing if not ambivalent. With the return of national defense to respectability in the 1980s, the 29th was again reactivated as the senior command of the Virginia and Maryland Guard units. It was designated a "light division," organized and equipped for mobility and rapid deployment, its helicopters probably costing more than the entire armament of the wartime division.

Attending the reactivation ceremony were a number of division veterans. I was among them, along with a long-time friend and war veteran, Marc Huet. The ceremony was held on the Fort Belvoir parade with considerable pomp, the two state governors and the secretary of the army extolling the past and the present 29th. As a finale, the troops passed in review.

I shall not try to assess the emotions of my fellow veterans as we watched the youthful soldiers, including women, march by; the familiar colors flying, and the band sounding out the stirring old marches. I noted that we were quiet, and some seemed preoccupied. I know that I was. For me, it was, vaguely, a reprise of parades long past with different uniforms and arms. Many in the marching ranks were of an age to be my grandchildren. Their black boots, mottled field dress and complicated-looking rifles were far removed from the brown-shoed, canvas-legginged, olive drab–uni-formed, and M-1 rifle–carrying troops of our day. Watching, I had the feeling of being a near, but not quite, stranger in a near, but not quite, strange place. The years had gone so fast and the changes were so drastic that there was no sorting it out in any order.

When the Stonewall Brigade returned to its Virginia National Guard armories, its colors with their twenty-four campaign streamers — four of which we had added — again had their place between the pictures of Robert E. Lee and Stonewall Jackson. Rank and file became again Virginian, but scattered across the Republic are men for whom the three-digit number, 116, must hold abiding significance and private memories. I am sure, also, that many have kept, along with dog tags, a small metal shield on which is enameled the heraldic device of a fleur-de-lis and a cross, all against a predominantly red background. Beneath is inscribed the motto "Ever Forward," not always a militarily sound tactic. Each element of the device represents a proud part of the regiment's history.

At first slowly, and now more rapidly, the wartime ranks are leached away. Some have had a delayed death from wounds; others still live with them. Only rarely, I observe, is pain shown, though it must be fairly constant. Time is sometimes more healing of emotional wounds than of physical ones. I find in those with whom I remain in touch the same tough resilience that so often in the war boosted my own flagging spirits. These may be generally classified as ordinary men; if so, they make of ordinary an ornament, and humankind more acceptable.

After demobilization, most Stonewallers went their private ways with their closely held memories. Still, a sizable number — including myself — joined the National Association of the 29th Division, organized into state departments and local posts; wives of members form auxiliaries. Regiments have separate associations, as do many companies and batteries. So, through a thousand reunions, memorial services, dedications, and battlefield pilgrimages, members hold in common thrall long-departed days, which, looked upon objectively, held so much of discomfort, boredom, frustration, and fear.

A society of masochists, we could be called, if this were all. But there is something more, overriding, unspoken, and that must be as old as war itself. I have tried to identify this as the heightened sense of having in youth stood together at the brink of the infinite and ultimate mystery — an experience of then-present dread, and now of abiding fascination. This perhaps touches it, but still inadequately, though I cannot say exactly why; it must, perhaps, go forever undefined and nameless.

As a final effort — probably equally foredoomed — I cite it as having faced one's frail and fully exposed self, and the selves of one's comrades, and finding, along with anguish and fear, something of value gained and given. It is this experience of shared vulnerability and its illuminations that cannot be forgotten, or in any final reckoning ever regretted.